"This book is a  thentic and genui reflects on her exp ulates so well as she speaks of her journey with her faith, her relationships with family, kids and close friends. The writing is so genuine and relatable as Simone shares her struggles, challenges, opportunities, insights, and learnings. There is something for everyone to gain in reading this book as it speaks to our experience as daughters, parents, friends and humans."

—Jennifer Lowrey,
Director of Youth Mental Health and Substance Use
Services

"This inspiring and uplifting life story offers beautiful lessons of parenting and how that harvested deep purpose and relationship with Jesus. *Life Lessons from the Car* is humorous, vulnerable, and full of wisdom. I could not put it down. So many moments of 'it's not just me who craves greater purpose'. Reading this book inspired me to make more room for the spirit in marriage and family life and open up to what may unfold next on my own spiritual journey."

—Tegan Smith, Entrepreneur and mother of three

"Simone Epplette's book, *Life Lessons from the Car*, beautifully weaves together elements of compassion, honesty, truth, surrender and humility to guide readers on a transformative journey towards fulfilment. Through her anecdotes, the author explores themes of her Christian faith, peace, love, healthy relationships, family, kindness, daily gratitude, strength, and compassion for others, making the book both relevant and healing for all readers. Epplette's narrative offers readers a path to freedom from anxiety and an anchored belief in forgiveness, kindness and unity, showcasing the power of faith and self-reflection in navigating life's challenges. This insightful and heartfelt book is a must-read for those seeking growth, spiritual enlightenment, and a deeper connection to themselves and others. *Life Lessons from the Car* is a beacon of hope and inspiration in a world that often feels dark and uncertain.

—David Glen Roberts, Husband,
Father of three, Vice President and Business Leader

LIFE
LESSONS
from the Car

Navigating Faith, Relationships and Fulfilment
While Reflecting on the Road to Living Your Best Life.

Simone Epplette

LIFE LESSONS FROM THE CAR
Copyright © 2025 by Simone Epplette

Unless otherwise indicated, scripture quotations are taken from THE HOLY BIBLE, NEW INTERNATIONAL VERSION®, NIV® Copyright © 1973, 1978, 1984, 2011 by Biblica, Inc.® Used by permission. All rights reserved worldwide. • Scripture quotations marked (AMP) are taken from the Amplified Bible, Copyright © 2015 by The Lockman Foundation, La Habra, CA 90631. All rights reserved. • Scripture quotations marked (ESV) are taken from The ESV® Bible (The Holy Bible, English Standard Version®). ESV® Text Edition: 2016. Copyright © 2001 by Crossway, a publishing ministry of Good News Publishers. The ESV® text has been reproduced in cooperation with and by permission of Good News Publishers. Unauthorized reproduction of this publication is prohibited. All rights reserved. • Scripture quotations marked (NKJV) are taken from the New King James Version®. Copyright © 1982 by Thomas Nelson. Used by permission. All rights reserved. • Scripture quotations marked (MSG) are taken from THE MESSAGE, copyright © 1993, 2002, 2018 by Eugene H. Peterson. Used by permission of NavPress. All rights reserved. Represented by Tyndale House Publishers, Inc.

Printed in Canada

ISBN: 978-1-4866-2632-8
eBook ISBN: 978-1-4866-2633-5

Word Alive Press
119 De Baets Street Winnipeg, MB R2J 3R9
www.wordalivepress.ca

Cataloguing in Publication information can be obtained from Library and Archives Canada.

DEDICATION

I started out writing this for my children. It was to be a book of life lessons that encouraged them to be part of the solution, part of the team—because at the end of the day, you have your relationships with God and each other, your experiences, your memories, and your fulfillment of purpose in this life to take with you for eternity in heaven. My love for you all is endless and infinite!

And now I'm writing it for God, my kids, their kids, and for the benefit of your kids. I desire to share my experiences and my learning through my relationships and circumstances!

CONTENTS

#LOVEPEOPLE
Buckle up—shifting gears with purpose!

"The purpose of a person's heart are deep waters, but one who has insight draws them out" (Proverbs 20:5).

Can we be better, more aligned, more fulfilled with our purpose? Can we be a kinder, more empathetic, forgiving, patient, energetic, productive, positive, and happier human race? Let's find out. The answer, or solution, lies within. It's really up to you. You have all the tools you need within you. You don't need to go searching outside of yourself. You simply need to tap into what you were created for and with. You have full control through the choices you make.

"*Be kind and helpful to one another, tender-hearted [compassionate, understanding], forgiving one another [readily and freely], just as God in Christ also forgave you*" (Ephesians 4:32, AMP).

My intention is to give you something to ponder, to help you learn and grow as a result, as I continue to do by sharing my journey. This book didn't turn out the way it started. God guided, and I trusted and followed! It has been years of picking up my writing and putting it back down, never feeling like it was complete, not knowing what this was for. But God knew, and He had a plan. And I was able to put it all together.

I write how I speak. I am not a novelist. I'd love to guide you to feeling complete. I wrote this for my children, for you, for me, for God, for your healthy relationships and fulfillment. At the end of this life, what's important is how you showed up from what you learned and how you grew through your relationships, experiences, and memories, and if you found fulfillment in those. This is all you take with you when you leave this earth! As you read this book, you'll discover what I believe to be most important. Maybe you already have an idea of what led me to being fully and completely fulfilled!

ACKNOWLEDGEMENTS

My mom constantly asks me if I'm writing, and she encourages me to continue. I'm grateful for her relentless and endless support and love in all that I do, always. I appreciate my dad and Renee for their constant prayers and their steadfast faith in Christ Jesus, and for reminding us around the Christmas dinner table in 2001 that we're called to be in community. They invited us to church, which began our true walk with God and our relationship with Jesus.

Becky Keen, my life coach, reminds me of who I am and how to get back to myself. She helped me set up my system to get this book done, and she made it clear who this book is for.

I'm grateful to Jennifer Kathleen for countless conversations that helped shape my writing. I appreciate her for her life-long friendship, her support no matter what the situation, her love, encouragement, and always, without fail, filling me up.

Christie, my dancing-through-life partner, for her loving texts and enthusiastic support. Helping me to breathe! Our walks and talks and quality time!

The Roberts family! The ten toes! Our walk by faith with this family took this book to new heights and has helped me understand the direction it needed to go. After years of picking it up and putting it down, not knowing how to bring it all together or what it was for, it all made sense and fell into place.

To my cousin Tegan, who helped me cross the finish line with this book when I was stuck in a pothole! For her unwavering support and encouragement when I thought I couldn't continue, and for her foundation of just projecting love.

Thanks to God for creating me with the personality, soul, and spirit to write this book, giving me the words to put to paper. I am grateful for my life group. They are relentless prayer warriors and supporters in all things, life with Jesus at the centre.

And, of course, my fearfully and wonderfully made children—Chelsey, Joel, and Hailey. I can't even express my love for who you all have become! You had to endure these life lessons over the years while trapped in the car, with no escape, listening and hopefully absorbing. For the endless memories and experiences! I learned and grew with the three of you! For the dancing, the cheering, the crying, the battling, your love, your strength, your loyalty, and your humour!

To my soulmate for eternity. Jonny, my husband, my partner, my leader, my co-pilot, God brought us together and has driven us through our journey and I feel beyond blessed that I got to do this life with you!

MY DISCLAIMER
Disclaimers pave the way for smooth driving!

"Therefore, having put away falsehood, let each one of you speak the truth with his neighbour, for we are members one of another" (Ephesians 4:25, ESV).

I am a strong, capable woman who believes in Jesus and His teachings. I often take on other people's stuff while attempting to help relieve them and make them feel better. I am hyper compassionate and aware of people's needs and emotions around me. I often try to make everyone feel as comfortable, welcomed, and loved as possible. I feel uncomfortable when people aren't comfortable. Maybe that's where it all stems from. I strongly dislike embarrassing anyone. I am an empathetic people pleaser who is sensitive to my surroundings. I'm also sensitive. I am extremely loyal, a fierce protector, and a mother bear to many cubs—mine, of course, all who have walked in and out of my life, and then all the underdogs.

I have a heart for the broken-minded around me and the ones I hear about. I'm drawn to the people who I feel need extra love, a little more grace, lots of guidance, added support, and, of course, what we all need—forgiveness. For example, if I hear about a car accident, my first sympathetic thought is for the person who caused the accident. I feel sad for the people who make mistakes that will cause them grief. I feel compelled to help them release this grief. Maybe this is my gift from God.

I can usually see the best in people trying to shine through, yet they continue to self-destruct. Sometimes, I must admit, my judgement can be clouded by their brokenness or their circumstances and can result in being too empathetic. I don't love victimism, (is that a word?). That's not what I am talking about.

I'm a wife with a thirty-plus-year loving relationship under my belt, a mom of three, a gramma, an office manager of over thirty years to a currently all-women staff, a friend, and a daughter who attends River Valley Vancouver Church.

I've done many types of workouts in my life: sports, aerobics, swimming, running, Pilates, yoga, weight training, various workout/training videos, hikes/walks, and many more. I completed the two-hundred-hour Vinyasa yoga teacher training course, and the fifty-hour Yin yoga teacher training, but never wanted to take up teaching. I just wanted to learn. I completed a life coaching course, but my only clients have been my husband, my kids, my dad, my mom, and a few friends here and there. I've had lots of failures and lots of successes. I'm not even close to perfect and am always learning.

I've experienced many challenges on my journey. I have battled and worked on eliminating anxiety, worry, and fear for most of my life. Here I will share my thoughts and experiences on how I believe you can be your best self on the road to wellness. Take what you need and leave the rest! My intention is for you to find out how you want to show up in this life, your purpose, and maybe what you actually need—things like genuine joy, laughter, releasing tears, kindness, compassion, love, happiness, gratitude, patience, motivation, forgiveness, giving, good health, healthy boundaries, and most importantly, a personal relationship with Jesus. My goal is to create our best life, with our truest self, and to be truly fulfilled!

The biggest truth I've discovered on my journey is that if you invite Jesus Christ into your heart, God will always be with you. Engage in a relationship with Him. Pray and cast all your cares and worries onto Him. I will give you scriptures throughout this book for you to reflect and meditate on. Scriptures to keep with you. Scriptures that helped me. Scriptures that will help you.

"*I can do all things though Christ who strengthens me*" (Philippians 4:13, NKJV).

I am on a journey to find my purpose and be fulfilled through God's will and plan for my life. I am not all these things all the time. I'm not perfect but continue to learn from my past mistakes and am working on growing into the person I was created to be.

We were created with a purpose in mind. Where do you think this purpose comes from? We were created to love and feel love. We thrive when we love and feel love. Where do you think this comes from? We were created to be in relationships. Why do we thrive when we have healthy relationships?

I am all about relationships and love and have been drawn to having a personal relationship with Jesus ever since I can remember. My mom was raised Anglican, and my dad, Catholic. As a child, my dad went to church with his mom, and my mom went with her parents. I remember going to Sunday school with my grandma, aka Granty. I loved it and her; I remember feelings of safety and warmth. I know now that the warmth is the love of Jesus and the presence of the Holy Spirit. The safety is His protection. I'm not even sure how many times she took me.

I'm blessed to have two parents who love me so much. I feel their love deeply! They love me as parents should love their children. They love me as Jesus loves you. I didn't grow up with any sort of religious background. Our little immediate family—my mom, my dad, and myself—didn't attend church. My dad and I would sometimes go to Christmas Eve mass and some random services, or maybe we just went once. I simply knew Jesus was who He said He was, and I believed in Him and that was that. I feel like I was born with my belief in Jesus. I don't think anyone could have convinced me that Jesus wasn't who He said He was. Of course, at that time, I didn't understand what it meant to have a relationship with Jesus or how to engage in it.

My parents gave me the space to believe what I believed and always supported me. My mom says I always had a strong faith, from the time I was little. They put me in a Christian daycare as a toddler. As I reflect on my journey now, this and the Sunday school likely sealed the deal in my belief in Jesus, or it was all in God's plan, chosen to walk with Him. I feel blessed and unworthy all at the same time. I feel sorrow for those who don't know or have a relationship with Christ. I want everyone to know and feel His love.

In elementary school, we recited the Lord's Prayer and sang the national anthem. I loved this. I never questioned it. I went to a Christian summer camp at age thirteen, right when I was becoming an out-of-control teen. I gave my life to Christ and by the grace of God was given salvation.

Salvation: preservation or deliverance from harm, ruin or loss (Oxford Languages definition). Salvation is God's grace. It's the gift of freedom from our sins that Jesus made possible by taking the punishment for our sins on the cross. It means to be saved or rescued by God from the consequences of our sins. You will then enter into a personal relationship with Jesus and have eternity with Him in heaven, and a guide for your lifetime here on earth.

> If you declare with your
> mouth, "Jesus is Lord,"
> and believe in your heart
> that God raised him from
> the dead, you will be

saved. For it is with your heart that you believe and are justified, and it is with your mouth that you profess your faith and are saved. As Scripture says, "Anyone who believes in him will never be put to shame." For there is no difference between Jew and Gentile—the same the Lord is Lord of all and richly blesses all who call on him, for, "Everyone who calls on the name the Lord will be saved." (Romans 10:9–13)

Again, the safety and warmth I felt was absolutely amazing! The love of the Holy Spirit was in me and around me. My spirit valve was wide open inside me, and I felt different. I felt the love of Christ. I felt the safety of His guidance and Him walking with me. When I returned home, I went to a new friend's house about an hour's drive away to attend a youth group. I loved the feeling of their home. Warm and safe! Holy Spirit was there. I wish I remembered her name to reconnect now.

I quit swearing for a few months after my return home from camp—*a few months* being the key words in that sentence. I could swear with the best of them. I wasn't an angel prior to going to camp or after my return, but I wasn't a complete jerk either. I guess that depends on who you ask. My mom would say I was a typical teen and I'm being too hard on myself. I was a pretty kind and loving kid. As I grew into a teen, I was angry, confused, hormonal, and had a careless attitude. The only things I truly cared about were my friends. Slowly I walked alone again. Thankfully, God and my family didn't give up on me.

At fifteen, I started going to church with my now husband, Jonn. Jonn's mom had started attending a local church, and she wanted to share God's love for us. She invited a wonderful man by the name of Rick Scott to come and chat with a few of Jonn's friends and me, his girlfriend at the time. We asked questions and got answers. Again, there was that safe, warm, loving feeling deep in my chest! I felt God's presence coming through Rick. I really loved those sessions with him. It felt like a break from the drama of teen life. In those meetings, none of that mattered. I truly felt the love of Jesus. Even in our brokenness, Jesus loved us. Jesus wanted to be part of our lives. He met us right where we were at. We all felt it, which led us to church.

We rolled in and sat in the very front row, wearing storm rider (jean) jackets. All the guys sported long, flowing mullets: business in the front, party in the back. I think the general congregation was a little shocked and also thrilled. The only one with the ability to get these teens through that door was God! No one else would have thought to invite us. Prior to this, you couldn't have dragged us in there. We were not the stereotypical church-attenders for that time. We didn't fit inside the box. But who did Jesus spend His time with? A prostitute, a tax collector, a zealot! Does He require you to wear your best outfit for Him to love you, to be in a relationship with you? Are you required to have your hair in a certain style? Does He even require you to be free from your addiction or sin? The answer is simply no! Jesus is happy to meet you right where you are this very second. Then you can work the rest out with Him as your guide.

Jonn and a few of the guys gave their lives to Christ; they were saved. Three of them, including Jonn, were baptized. I did not get baptized at that time.

I can't remember how long we went to church for. I don't think it was long. Our thought was, *Awesome* (or maybe it was) *choice, we have salvation*. We knew we were going to heaven and not hell. It's all that mattered.

We went on to live our lives how we wanted to live them, which was not in a "holy" way. It's like we did a pit stop for Jesus and filled up with the Holy Spirit. We felt amazing and were off and running the race alone again, living in the flesh, doing what we wanted to do. Self-focused, self-centred, self-destructive! This did not serve us well in any way. As I said, I wasn't raised in the church, at least not one that I remember. I'd never read the Bible, so at the time, I didn't understand what it meant to walk with God. I learned this later. I simply always knew that Jesus was with me and in my heart. No matter where you go, He never gives up on you and will always forgive you if you truly repent of your sins. Does this mean you'll go on to live a perfect life without angst, without sin? No, it doesn't!

I never understood the rules of religion. Honestly, I still don't. I don't think of myself as "religious." My faith is super simple: God is love. He's a personal being who created us to have a personal relationship with Him. He gave us free will to either engage in that relationship or not. What you put into this personal relationship is your choice, much like every other relationship. No one can force you into a relationship. You make a choice. You have a choice to live with Him in heaven for eternity or live separate from Him.

God is light and love. You can't get into heaven just by doing good works. This is like paying someone to be your friend. What if God said that if you spend fifty hours a month volunteering, then you can go to heaven? That would take away your choice to have the relationship because you want it. What if I don't do any volunteer work but my partner spends all their time serving? Do I not get to go? What if I donate money but not time? Who measures this? Good works aren't required. Is it amazing to do good works? Absolutely, 100 per cent yes! But what is the measure of good works? How many good works are enough? I believe everyone gets a chance to go to heaven. Everyone can make a choice to call out to God in their final moments, and I truly believe lots do. Many people in the world don't even hear about Jesus.

God didn't create sin. He gave us a choice, but we humans sinned. He loves us so much that He sent His one and only son to show us His love and to pay the price for our sin. His blood was shed for your salvation so that you can spend eternity in heaven. Jesus paid your debt, like if a judge paid the fine for someone else's crime and told them they were free to go. What you do with this is up to you.

"As the body without the spirit is dead, so faith without deeds is dead!" (James 2:26).

My work has always been to merge my true Christian self with my secular world. I have not done this well at all! I have a goal and am on a road to be aligned with who I am and was created to be, trusting God's will and purpose for my life. I believe that I am to be a woman of faith, including all the things I have mentioned, in a loving relationship with Jesus and projecting that love to the people around me. I fell away from this for a time when I felt the pressure of the world closing in. It's not easy or struggle-free to be a Christian.

My writing is fully inclusive. No one is excluded; this is for you whether you're a Christian or not! This book can help everyone from anywhere. It's for people who feel like something is missing, people who are seeking after things of the earth but still find themselves unhappy or unfulfilled. People with broken or unhealthy relationships. People who deal with anxiety and fear. People who have accumulated lots of stuff but feel empty and keep trying to fill life with more stuff and desires of the flesh but never feel fulfilled or joyful. It's for people who are broken by their circumstances or their past. People who are searching or feel lost, and those who don't even realize they're lost. It's for people who want to teach our next generation about love, relationships, and choices. And most definitely, it's for our youth, to guide them into adulthood with great coping skills. It's for people who like to think, ponder, and/or journal. For people who want to be filled with love and joy. For people who don't have it all together but want to teach the next generation. Everyone is welcome!

I don't sit in judgement of your past or where you're currently at. That's not my job or purpose.

> Do not judge, or you too will be judged. For in the same way you judge others, you will be judged, and with the measure you use, it will be measured to you. Why do you look at the speck of sawdust in your brother's eye and pay no attention to the plank in your own eye? How can you say to your brother, "Let me take the speck out of your eye," when all the time there is a plank in your own eye? (Matthew 7:1–4)

TAKE TIME
to be still, reflect, listen, journal, and pray.

What aspects of your life do you feel are in need of greater alignment as you journey toward personal growth and fulfillment? What experiences or relationships have shaped your understanding of love, compassion, and forgiveness?

_____

_____

_____

_____

_____

_____

_____

_____

_____

_____

_____

_____

_____

_____

_____

_____

_____

_____

_____

_____

_____

_____

_____

_____

PRAY

Lord, guide me to be
transparent and authentic
today. Help me to grow
and find fulfillment in
your purpose. Amen

USEFUL TOOLS
Your Roadside Repair Kit

*"Do not merely listen to
the word, and so deceive
yourselves. Do what it says"*
(James 1:22).

SKILLS TO WORK WITH AS YOU NAVIGATE YOUR LIFE

These are the conversations I have with my children, life lessons in the car, driving from one activity to the next. When they have no choice but to hear me talk. When they spill their guts over situations or decisions in their lives. Or when we congregate around the island in the kitchen or sit on the edge of their bed. They tell me that I turn everything into a life lesson! Some of this is the stuff I didn't get to tell them because they were teens. If you've parented teens, then enough said—

you know what I'm talking about. I've learned that you need to keep it short and to the point. Okay, maybe I haven't put this entirely into practice yet! It's those times when you had more to say and you wanted desperately to continue the conversation, but you saw your teen's eyes start to glaze over as they nodded, and you knew they were no longer listening.

Life Lesson: I've been hit in the head a few times in my life. ☺ I'm not even joking! God has more plans for me on earth, and I believe His angels have been protecting me all along: "*Are not all the angels ministering spirits sent out [by God] to serve [accompany, protect] those who will inherit salvation?[Of course they are!]*" (Hebrews 1:14 AMP).

More learning, growing, and aligning are required before my time's up here. These things are what I have learned and tried to grow from. Things I've heard and tried to put into practice. Things I was reminded of and tried to retain for the next time. Things God put in front of me that I have chosen to focus on.

Just for fun, here is the short versions of these stories.

Once when I was nine years old, a boy in my hood and I were battling with words back and forth. Then he threw a big boulder toward me, which unintentionally hit me in the head. I think he was just as shocked as I was that he had such good aim. This resulted in a large lump above my eye. I'm sure the "boulder" was more like a large rock, but at the time, it seemed huge! The boy's mom brought him over to apologize, and before I opened the door, I parted my bangs so he could see the goose egg he'd created. My mom promptly replaced my bangs over the lump so that it wasn't as visible. She said he already felt bad enough, and we shouldn't punish him by making him feel worse. Thanks, Mom! I really appreciated that, and it started to shape who I am today! Compassion and forgiveness were taught at an early age. I have fond memories of our childhood in that neighbourhood and feel a bond toward him.

Another time, I experienced "the old baseball bat to the side of the head." I might have been ten or eleven years old. Lesson learned: don't stand behind your friend when they're throwing the ball up in the air to hit it. A miss is possible! Result? Huge black eye!

A couple of years later, when I was twelve and visiting a friend in Alberta, I was riding a horse and fell off; the horse stepped on my head (not the horse's fault). I don't remember all the events that led up to that. I think I tried to jump a small ditch with the horse, but that could be my sensationalized version of the story! The doctor said I was lucky to be alive. Another black eye! This time the wonderful family I stayed with gave me a large steak to place on my eye. This was a fun memory for me. I remember nothing else from that trip!

When I was fourteen, I went skiing at Grouse Mountain. The snow was coming down hard and hitting us head on. The fog was thick, and we couldn't see very far ahead. We decided to call it a day with one last run toward the lodge. Wearing my super cool pink sunglasses and white Sunice jacket, I hit a chair lift tower. I broke my jaw and was again lucky or blessed to be alive.

Life Lesson: Wear a helmet and goggles! I'm thankful this became a thing once my kids started snowboarding—likely due to many people like me, and some not as fortunate to come out unscathed.

God doesn't promise a life without speed bumps and pot holes (on the head or otherwise), or pain, suffering, or grief. We will undoubtedly go through trials and tribulations. God doesn't cause the trials or suffering, but He may allow you to walk through them. If we didn't, we wouldn't get the opportunity to seek after Him and learn and grow. God promises that if you believe He's your Lord and Saviour, and you invite Him into your heart, He will walk with you, guide you, and even carry you every step of the way.

Did you know that God has 8,810 promises for us in the Bible? That's more than one for every hour of every day in a year!

WHO CAUSES OUR SUFFERING?

Why do bad things happen to good people? Like say, when people are praying and they're asking for healing and sometimes they don't get that healing. The number one reason people would say they do not believe in God is, I can't believe in God 'cause there is suffering in the world. If you do not believe in God because there's suffering in the world, ok, let's just say there is no God. Is there still suffering and the answer is yes. So, if suffering exists and there is no God, then where does suffering come from? Most suffering comes from humans hurting each other. So why do we hold God accountable

for what we do to each
other? And so, here's why
bad things happen to good
people, because it's a broken world and suffering
and pain are real.[1]

"*The Lord himself goes before you and will be with you;
he will never leave you nor forsake you. Do not be afraid; do
not be discouraged*" (Deuteronomy 31:8). Pray, pray, pray,
pray, pray, pray, pray your way through everything! Jesus
wants to be part of every aspect of your life. He's all about
love and having a relationship with you. Your prayers don't
need to be long, eloquent, wordy literary masterpieces. He
does give this beautiful gift to many prayer warriors, but
if this isn't you, that's totally okay! He loves to hear the
simplest of prayers.

I used to pray much less because I felt my prayers were
too simple. Wrong! Limiting belief! I felt like, "God, you
created me to be a strong, capable woman. I've got this.
I can go it alone, so go ahead and help others who have
greater needs than mine." Wrong again! God wants to
connect with everyone exactly where they're at. I like to

---

[1] McManus, Erwin (@erwinmcmanus). Instagram post. September 25, 2023.
ttps://www.instagram.com/reel/CxoaKeZPeWg/?igsh=MXE5ZTRrcWF-
0dHhhZA==.

reframe it as, "I am a prayer warrior, just in a minimal word kind of way." I'm learning and growing into being bold in my prayers and to pray through everything.

Growing up, I did pray, but very randomly and about random things. I now know that praying is a practice you choose and grow from. I'm embarrassed to say that in my teen years, I prayed for things like, "God, please make the bed stop spinning, and I'll never drink again!" Because He's a grace-filled, merciful God, He always answered those prayers. And there were many times I prayed that prayer. Alcohol and I were not, and still are not, friends! It took me into my thirties to really dial this back and get the hint. I never was able to drink large amounts, but that didn't stop me from trying. Sure, I enjoy having drinks now too, but in total moderation and usually only socially. My body doesn't accept alcohol well. I often felt sick when I drank. There have been times when I didn't drink at all, or when I had a few at a social event. Then there were the times that the alcohol clouded my judgement and I got wrapped up in the moment and had more than I should have. More often than not, those times didn't go well for me.

God is a personal being! He wants a relationship with you. He wants you to pray through every situation, every trial, every bump, and every moment of your life—the good, the bad, the ugly. This builds your relationship with Him! Communication is a key factor to building successful relationships, so why not with God too?

I believe that with prayer, quantity is better than quality. Quality is a wonderful and beautiful gift, but it's not required. ☺

> Do not be anxious about anything, but in every situation, by prayer and petition, with thanksgiving, present your requests to God. And the peace of God, which transcends all understanding, will guard your hearts and your minds in Christ Jesus.
> (Philippians 4:6–7)

TAKE TIME

to be still, reflect, listen, journal, and pray.

When reflecting on your life experiences, can you see the teachable moments? Write down a specific memory and the lesson it taught you.

_____

_____

_____

_____

_____

_____

_____

_____

_____

_____

_____

_____

_____

_____

_____

_____

_____

_____

_____

_____

PRAY

God, thank you for your
consistent promises.
Please walk with me and
talk with me, guide me
and direct me toward
your purpose and plan for
my life. Help me to feel
the peace of your presence
as I navigate the trials of
my life. Amen!

BUILDING FULFILLMENT
Jesus, Take the Wheel!

*"By wisdom a house is
built, and through under-
standing it is established;
through knowledge its
rooms are filled with rare
and beautiful treasures"*
(Proverbs 24:3–4).

The ultimate achievement is to be truly fulfilled! Throughout this book, I'll share how you can become truly fulfilled simply through your own choices.

I believe that:
- a personal relationship with Jesus,
- mental- and self-wellness,
- healthy relationships, and
- physical wellness

are the rock-solid foundations on which you can build your fulfillment.

"*This is My commandment, that you love and unselfishly seek the best for one another, just as I have loved you*" (John 15:12, AMP).

You are in control! You can only control yourself and how you react and interact. Reflect on who you want to be, how you want to show up and live your life, how you want to show up in your current and future relationships, and if you want to take action toward fulfillment!

> "Life is 10% of what happens to me and 90% of how I react to it."[2] — Chuck Swindoll

I will share with you some tools that have helped me. Remember, you have all you need. You just need to tap into what you already have. I too have needed reminders. I've learned these things through my personal relationship with Jesus and through my own experiences working through anxiety, raising three kids, being a wife and a career woman and die-hard supporter of my entire family. I've learned these tools from the Word of God, life coaches (my personal fav

[2] "Charles R. Swindoll Quotes," BrainyQuote, accessed November 1, 2024, https://www.brainyquote.com/quotes/charles_r_swindoll_388332.

is Becky Keen), mentors, motivators, Christian influences/pastors (like Joyce Meyer, Cliffe Kenchtle, and many more), public speakers, family, and friends. I've learned things from my mom, who learned from her mom. I've experienced life with one of my favourite people, Jennifer Kathleen, who works in the field of mental health and has been my longest life-time friend. I talk to her about all this stuff.

As I wrote many of these chapters, prior to my starfish moment (more on that later), and as I dove into His Word, I had a massive realization. As Oprah says, that "aha moment!" Here's the thing: God said all these things that I talk about in this book first! He is all these things! He is love! God gives us all these tools in scripture that coaches, counsellors, and motivators are saying today and have said in the past! The Bible was the first self-help book!

This is so interesting and absolutely amazing! All I write about is written right there in the Bible. My favourite version is *The Everyday Life Bible, Amplified Version*, featuring comments and notes by Joyce Meyer. It's like having Joyce with you while you read God's Word. Your own personal pastor giving perspective on various scriptures. I love this!

Jesus' teachings are just common sense to me. It feels like the natural order of things, and I know it all comes from God. This makes sense, right? Jesus is the way, the truth, and the life (John 14:6). In the Word of God, Jesus teaches us how to treat each other with kindness, compassion, and love. He talks about fear, anxiety, worry, forgiveness, relationships, boundaries, courage, faith, control, healing, insecurity, hope, humility, grace, integrity, peace, joy, love, stress, patience, wisdom, and mindfulness. You'll find all the tools you need to get through life in His Word. Wow, just wow! God is the creator of all things. He created us in His own image. He knows our minds, our soul, our spirit. He knows every hair on your body. We need that connection with Him to completely fulfill our purpose and His plan for our lives because we were created to worship.

TAKE TIME
to be still, reflect, listen, journal, and pray.

What foundations are you building your fulfillment on?
What are you worshipping? Is it fulfilling?

_____

_____

_____

_____

_____

_____

_____

_____

_____

_____

_____

_____

_____

_____

_____

_____

_____

_____

_____

_____

PRAY

Dear Lord, please help me
to worship you alone and
not things of the flesh.
Help me to tap into your
teachings and clearly see
the things that are most
important.
Thank you, Jesus! Amen!

PHYSICAL WELLNESS
Keep Revving Your Engine

"Beloved, I pray that all
may go well with you and
that you may be in good
health, as it goes well with
your soul" (3 John 1:2,
ESV).

Your body is your vessel, your mode of transportation. You get one per lifetime! It takes you where you want to go physically, so it's important to take care of it like any other mode of transport.

Your mind is the controller of said vessel. You have control of you—you are in charge of your wellness, both physical and mental. Your mind is the driver of your vehicle, the pilot of your plane, the surfer of your wave, the jockey on your horse, the sailor of your ship. You control how you will drive your car or steer your ship, fly your plane, ride your wave, or run your horse. Only you can do this for yourself. And when you do, the mental health benefits of this will give you great strength in all aspects of your life, both mentally and physically!

Your mode of transportation needs proper energy to run well and function, much like your own body. Have it serviced regularly, and check in daily. Do you have enough gas, oil, fluid? Top it up! Are your interior and exterior clean? Air it out! Flush it out!

Fuel or nourish your body properly to give it energy and build it up. Make it walk or run; get your heart pumping daily to release endorphins to make it strong and durable to carry you through a long life. Detoxify it, practise good personal hygiene, give it loving care, and give it a break through rest and sleep. (This is a constant work in progress for me.) Most importantly, let it breathe!

NOTE: Kids! Brushing your teeth regularly has many benefits. Oral health and good personal hygiene are important to your physical and mental health—not to mention the people around you. I can't stress this enough. You won't regret taking care of your teeth. I'm pretty sure my kids are sick of hearing it from me! And no, I don't work in the dental industry!

Do you want more energy, more fulfillment, more joy? Start gaining these things through moving. You don't have to be a full-out athlete, track star, or even coordinated to gain all the benefits of physical activity. There are many activities to choose from. I'm not a strong runner. I've never been a runner at all, and when I could no longer run due to physical limitations, after forcing myself to try to become a runner, I started hot yoga.

Another disclaimer: As a true and faithful follower of Jesus, my every yoga practice was with Him. I prayed to start, I prayed throughout, and I prayed in gratitude when I made it through. I never bought into or worshipped any other religion associated with ancient yoga practices. I still don't know the history of yoga, as I've never focused it. I use the movement of yoga as an exercise for my body through my spiritual connection with Christ.

I know that some people question how you can practise yoga and be a Christian. I absolutely did! When I took my yoga teacher training, I didn't know the history. Honestly, when we had the class about the history, I felt sick, and I really struggled with it. I came home and shed a few tears. I feel strongly about my faith, and I didn't want God to think that I wasn't all about Him. I am fiercely loyal. I talked to my husband about it and prayed about it.

Our class had a big debate/discussion, which at one point got heated, as there were a few Christians taking the training. In the end we agreed that yoga is about your own practice and journey, and you can believe what you want to believe. I believe God put this on my heart. My journey revolves around a relationship with Jesus, so that's who I brought with me to class.

I love the slow, methodical movement. I love the stillness. I love the peace. I love the heat. I love the breathing. I love the exercise. I love the time I spend with God, and I love that it's not about anyone else in the room. It's simply time for me to enhance my relationship with myself. I wasn't doing it for anybody else.

I am constantly changing in my faith and my growth as a person.

Anything that elevates your heart rate, even slightly, will increase your quality of life. It doesn't have to cost you anything either. At any fitness level you can start. Start gradually or jump in. Go and enjoy our great outdoors! Outdoors can be found everywhere and is free for all. Breathe fresh air! A walk will fill you up with more energy and endorphins. If you don't love traditional exercise, be creative. What else can you do to elevate your heart rate? Maybe renovation projects around the home? Maybe refinishing old furniture?

Maybe cleaning your home in a vigorous way? Maybe intimate time with your spouse? Maybe yard work?

> "Nothing is impossible, the word itself says I'm possible."[3]
> —Audrey Hepburn

I did play sports and was a somewhat active child/teen. I also took brisk walks with my mom. I walked a lot as a teen, as we lived a way from our town centre. Jennifer Kathleen and I would power walk along the dyke that connected us to our town. To get home in time for curfew, we'd got fast!

I woke up at twenty-eight years old, newly pregnant with thirty extra pounds of fat, not muscle. That's when I made the choice to be active as an adult. When Jonn and I got married, I was so excited to buy whatever junk food I wanted. Growing up in my house, ginger ale, popcorn, and digestive cookies were a total treat. I'm still a popcorn junkie to this day! I don't blame my mother for this, but it's a generational thing. She was, and still would be if she could be, a popcorn addict. I appreciate my parents'

---

[3] "Audrey Hepburn Quotes," BrainyQuote, accessed November 1, 2024, https://www.brainyquote.com/quotes/audrey_hepburn_413479.

healthy food choices for me now that I'm an adult. It has truly shaped my food choices today. As a child, I envied the kids who had Wagon Wheels[4] and sugared cereal in their food pantry. I went a little crazy with my food choices when I got married. I made small, manageable changes once I regained my senses.

I was done with scheduled sports. I started brisk walking with a friend. It felt amazing, both mentally and physically. Find a walking, running, workout, biking, or whatever activity you love partner. It doesn't always have to be the same person; you could have a list of people. My walking partner at the time was a friend who was also pregnant, so we had lots to talk about and could support each other. We scheduled our walk times. My mind was better. My mood was better. I ate better. I slept better. Walking was the beginning of my lifestyle change. I highly recommend an active buddy or accountability partner. I've had many different walking partners over the years. They motivate you and give you someone to motivate, which is a no brainer for feeling good. You'll get more than just physical benefits from this. You'll be building relationships! To this day I use walking as a form of connecting with my friends and family.

---

[4] A cookie crust and marshmallow dessert covered with chocolate.

Life gets busy! It's not always possible to fit in events, dinners, or things that take a lot of time. But my relationships are important to me. To this day, one of my besties, Christie, and I walk our dogs and get caught up. We walk fast and talk the same way, filling up on each other's lives, offering up support, validation, and love. Even though we may not see each other socially that much, we have a deep connection because we take the time for each other, even if it's just for a walk. Building our relationship and connection!

The same is true with God. Spend time with God by reading the Bible, walking and talking, praying, being still, and meditating. The more time you spend, the more connected you'll feel.

Weight training started after I had my second child. It happened during one of those middle-of-the-night feedings. I saw an infomercial, and it actually changed my/our fitness life. I should do a commercial. Never had I ever ordered anything from an infomercial, and definitely not at 3:00 a.m. I told Jonn the next day that I'd ordered the P90X program! He was a great sport about it and jumped on board with me. We've completed that program together a few times. This was also the start of us working out together and the beginning of many other fitness programs that would follow over the years. It was easy to fit these workouts into our already super busy schedule. We just did the workout at 5:00 a.m. Again, we started with small changes.

After we completed this program, we started to build an at-home gym by buying a few items at a time. Hand-held weights, exercise bands, and other gym accessories were often birthday or Christmas gifts to each other. With two kids, it wasn't realistic or in the budget to pay for childcare while we worked out. We were more efficient with our time working out at home or taking the kids on a walk or run in their stroller. To this day, we still work out, walk, bike, paddle board, and golf together. Of course, life happens and gets hectic, and things drop off or slide, but we push each other. I can be competitive, so if I hear Jonn in the gym when I chose to roll over in bed, I think, *Crap, he's getting a workout in.* I can't handle that, so I hop out of bed, change quickly, and get into our gym. If he says he's busy and isn't going to work out in the morning, I'll think, *Okay, I'll take a day off, or I'll do something else later.* But if he ends up in the gym, I'm like, "What are you doing? I thought you weren't going to work out."

He just laughs and says, "I changed my mind." Then I go get my gear on, because for some reason, I think I'm missing out! He finds this extremely funny. Maybe I have a problem!

Okay, I can admit it—I'm a competitive person, but not generally with other people. Usually it's just with myself or when I'm teamed up with my man. When we were on vacation in Mexico, the resort had a couples competition night as part of the entertainment. We thought we were going to kick butt! It was comprised of relay races/games. Jonn and I are pretty great competitive partners. Really, we are just great partners! We work well as a team. If we had lost, which we didn't, we would have been fine with it. I don't need to win when I'm playing for myself. But when Jonn and I team up for something as partners, we give it our all and get competitive, but we have no problem conceding when a loss seems imminent.

Being on the same team and working together can really bond you with your partner and build your relationship! You can team up in a lot of areas, everything from being loyal to each other, to parenting, to faith, to finances, to common goals and interests, to the direction you want your family to go in. Check in, communicate, and negotiate all of these.

Jonn and I have been building our God muscles together, which my personal favourite. This is also a disciplined training that fills you with strength, purpose, peace, and joy.

I am competitive with myself. I have a fictitious activity bank account. I deposit my activity into my account and withdraw my sedentary time. I assess how much time I relax against how much activity or work I exert. If I'm filled up with active time, then I can relax more, and it feels amazing! This works well for me, as I give myself permission to relax. Otherwise, I would not! I need to work at stopping before I'm exhausted or simply drop. If my bank account is low on activity, then not only does my body feel off, but so does my mind. I saw a meme once that said, "My husband and I laugh about how competitive we are … but I laugh more!

Fun Fact: Is it true what they say—"You are what you eat"? I believe it to be true, but my son disagrees. When he was a child, I used to tell him he was going to turn into a cereal bar. He found this quite comical, as he hadn't heard the saying. As he grew into a teenager, I said he was going to turn into Kraft Dinner. FYI, he never turned into any of these things! So maybe he's right! But he was diagnosed with ulcerative colitis and had to have his large intestine removed. Is it related? It's a factor for sure! Stress is the biggest factor, and when you add processed foods to the mix, it certainly doesn't work with your body to heal you.

"So then, whether you eat or drink or whatever you do, do all to the glory of [our great] God" (1 Corinthians 10:31,

AMP). Calories in versus energy out is one formula, but if all you eat is fast, processed, sugar-filled, refined carbs, you'll have low energy and possibly harm how your body functions (heart, liver, kidneys, intestines). If you eat the same calories but in nutritious, natural options, you'll feel cleaner and have more energy, enhancing your bodily functions that give you good energy. It will enhance your heart health, brain function, and mood, and it will help to prevent cancer and other diseases. The vitamins in these foods will nourish all your internal organs.

I'm not a nutritional scientist or a doctor, but God gave us all we need on earth to sustain us. It makes sense that if God didn't create it and it can't be grown and eaten from the earth, then our bodies don't know how to process it. They essentially turn processed or genetically modified foods into waste, which turns into toxins and disease in our body and/or unwanted extra fat in our arteries. This harms our optimal body function.

God provided us with "super foods," and they are worth some research!

A healthy diet will require a lifestyle change, as it's not a short-term goal. Although there are benefits to cleanses and fasting, they're not a means to control your eating habits. (Jonny, my love!)

The goal is to be healthy physically, inside and out. I'm not talking about being a fitness influencer. Do this for your body health, not for your body image. We all come in different, beautiful shapes and sizes. If we all looked the same, you wouldn't be you. So embrace your beautiful self and treat yourself as you would treat someone you truly loved. This is a form of loving yourself.

If you have physical limitations, seek professional help for ideas, and see your doctor. YouTube has a wealth of physical activity ideas, but make sure you check with your physician first. I am not a personal training professional, so make sure you get sound advice for your body type.

TAKE TIME

to be still, reflect, listen, journal, and pray.

What are some small, manageable changes you can make
to prioritize more physical wellness in your daily life?
What physical activities do you enjoy? Are there any new
ones you'd like to try? Who can you partner with?

_____

_____

_____

_____

_____

_____

_____

_____

_____

_____

_____

_____

_____

_____

_____

_____

_____

_____

_____

PRAY

Lord, help me to honour
the body you gave me.
Guide me to nourish it
and love it as you do.
Help motivate me to be
as active as my physical
ability allows. Heal me of
anything hindering this.
Amen!

CHOICES AND FOCUS
Steer your thoughts.
Navigate your destiny!

*"Finally, brothers and
sisters, whatever is true,
whatever is noble, whatever
is right, whatever is pure,
whatever is lovely, whatever
is admirable—if anything
is excellent or praisewor-
thy—think about such
things"* (Philippians 4:8).

You decide! You have a choice! Let your circumstances control you *or* you control your circumstances. Your reaction to your circumstances is within your control. You are not a victim of your circumstances:

> "Your present circumstances don't determine where you can go; they merely determine where you start."[5]
> —Nido Qubein

Your choices affect your fulfillment; you can decide how and where your life will go. Your life direction is up to you. You don't need to know where you will end up. Move through life living in the present but looking to achieve your future goals and dreams.

What you focus on will grow! Visualizing can be a powerful tool. Many people use this in sports, for example. In a study on the power of visualization in basketball, conducted by Dr. Biasiotto in 1996 at the University of Chicago (maybe you've heard of it), students were divided into three groups and tested on how many free throws they could successfully complete. Group One practised free throws for half an hour every day for the thirty days. Group Two came to the gym, closed their eyes, and visualized themselves making free throws for half an hour each day for thirty days, but they didn't touch a basketball. Group Three was told not to touch a basketball or practise

---

[5] "Nido Qubein Quotes," BrainyQuote, accessed November 1, 2024, https://www.brainyquote.com/quotes/nido_qubein_178331.

or play for thirty days. After the thirty days, he tested them again. Group One improved 24 per cent, Group Two improved 23 per cent , and Group Three didn't improve at all (not surprisingly).

This study doesn't suggest that visualization should replace physical work or practice; instead, it shows the power of focus and directing your thoughts. Positive visualization in conjunction with physical practice can produce better results.

Visualizing success helps you to believe in it.

> Then the Lord answered me and said, "Write the vision and engrave it plainly on [clay] tablets so that the one who reads it will run. For the vision is yet for the appointed [future] time. It hurries toward the goal [of fulfillment]; it will not fail. Even though it delays, wait [patiently] for it, because it will certainly come; it will not delay." (Habakkuk 2:2–3, AMP)

When you focus on the negativity in your life, that is exactly what you'll find! You can always find people who have wronged you, or disappointing situations. It's easier to see and focus on these things. Negativity is a powerful suppressant. Did you know that 70 to 80 per cent of our thoughts are negative. Yikes! The good news is that we can work on reframing our thoughts and turning them positive. The positives or blessings, the things you can be grateful for, are also available to focus on, and you can choose them as your focus. It's a practice. Keep choosing it and choosing it and choosing it until you actually feel it! Your thoughts are a choice. You have a say in where you let your mind go. It's not always easy! Fake it till you make it! Visualize! Manifest!

"Your thoughts direct your path." Thank you, Jennifer Kathleen! So very true!

You manifest what you focus on. If you focus on negativity or unhappiness, then you will experience negativity and unhappiness. Focus on it and it will grow. This rings true for both achievement/success and demise/failure.

> "You cannot have a positive
> life and a negative mind."
> —Joyce Meyer (*Battlefield
> of the Mind*)[6]

[6] Joyce Meyer Quotes, BrainyQuote, accessed November 12, 2024, https://www.brainyquote.com/quotes/joyce_meyer_567542.

You have an internal world and an external world. If you find peace and fulfillment in the internal world (mind), you'll have a different perspective on the external world.

"*I have told you these things, so that in me you may have peace. In this world you will have trouble. But take heart! I have overcome the world*" (John 16:33). If you haven't already, invite Jesus into your heart to walk through life with you. When you do, you'll be fulfilled with peace, positivity, love, and joy! I'm saving the best for last! More on this later! If you haven't asked Him for salvation and you feel like you can't read another word without Him, I am beyond elated for you. Jump to the chapter on salvation in this book and then jump back!

Reframe your thoughts from limiting beliefs to positive, empowering beliefs. Find something positive in a negative situation or turn the negative into a positive. Take your thoughts captive and reframe them before they become a fear or produce anxiety that causes you to spiral downwards. Don't let it consume you. Notice that it's just a thought. Tell yourself that you will not engage with the thought, that you will not entertain or spend any time with the thought. Give yourself permission to let it go. Capture the thought, crumple it into a little ball, and toss it to God. If this is a repeating thought, you can continue to cast it out and reject it over and over again. You can also stop and ask yourself if it's a true story and then reframe it if it isn't.

My thought: *No one wants to read your book!*

Question: Is this a true story?

Answer: No, it's not. My family and friends have all said they are eager to read it. They are not nobody! My thought is not true, and I can capture it, not spiral on it or engage in it. I won't' give it any weight but will let it go. Crumple up or capture the thought and cast it out to God.

> casting all your cares [all your anxieties, all your worries, and all your concerns, once and for all] on Him, for He cares about you [with deepest affection, and watches over you very carefully].
>
> (1 Peter 5:7, AMP)

TAKE TIME

to be still, reflect, listen, journal, and pray.

Do you have negative thoughts that you can reframe before they spiral into fear or anxiety? Are these recurring thoughts? How can you change that pattern? What are these thoughts? Ask yourself, "Is this a true story?"

_____

_____

_____

_____

_____

_____

_____

_____

_____

_____

_____

_____

_____

_____

_____

_____

_____

_____

PRAY

God, remind me to keep
a positive mind and not
focus or ruminate on
negative thoughts. Lord,
I capture these thoughts
and toss them out. I know
that you don't want me to
dwell on these, as they do
not serve me. Give me the
strength to do so. Thank
you for your grace and
peace! Amen!

ACTIVELY PERSONAL
Keep Your Motor Running!

"But those who hope in the Lord will renew their strength. They will soar on wings like eagles; they will run and not grow weary, they will walk and not be faint" (Isaiah 40:31).

The majority of my choices and most of my focus have revolved around raising, supporting, and giving everything I am to my family. I made a decision long ago to live a fairly active lifestyle. I say "fairly" because I'm not an extremist. I needed this lifestyle to stay at the energy level required to raise three kids, work full-time, and be a loving and supportive partner.

I grew up with an active family. I don't mean that we went on family runs or worked out every day, but my dad played soccer and squash and skied, and he was always busy with a house project or renovating houses to flip. I skied from a young age, and my mom walked—and I don't mean strolled. She brisked her way through life! I usually loved going with her, except when I was a teen and needed an excessive amount of sleep or social time with my friends.

I played sports right through to the teen years, when I took an aerobics class and played soccer and softball. Okay, maybe I didn't take many aerobics classes, and I feel like there was a big gap in my soccer years, and I'm pretty sure that softball collapsed because our teenage coaches didn't show up to practice! I think my parents' version of this would be that my social schedule as a teen was far more important than any organized sports! My mom and dad are doers and so were their parents. There is that apple and the tree again! I am definitely not a sitter by nature, but my parents would tell a different story about how Jennifer Kathleen and I slept in the back seat of the car all through the amazingly scenic Europe trip they took us on at fifteen years old!

In my twenties I went back to soccer, went to Whistler one weekend, and started a ladies' soccer team with my husband as our coach. I did this until my oldest child was about two. My husband and I had played slo-pitch since we were nineteen, but is that really physical? It was more like a drinking arm workout. But we created the best memories! And it was great for mental health!

When I became pregnant with my oldest at twenty-eight and got physical at my three-month mark, I just about fell off the table when the doctor told me that I was in poor physical condition. I changed my mindset back to my roots and started by simply brisk walking with my friend Pam, who was pregnant with her second. Walking was easy and felt good. It got my blood pumping and filled me with endorphins, so I was rewarded physically right away. I had watched my mom do it with her friends, which was positive role modeling. My mom has modeled so many positive things in my life; it brought her joy and physical wellness, so this was easy for me to incorporate.

Soon this wasn't enough, so I added home workout videos, then running, then classes, then weight training, then yoga, and all sorts of other things in between. Soon I adjusted my food intake because I realized that processed or fast food wasn't serving me, and it didn't feel good to eat it anymore. I changed small things, things that were easy to drop from my personal menu. I do eat unhealthy food for sure, but I aim for moderation. I don't always hit the target. I make food choices all the time, to this day. I'll eat a healthy dinner option then have dessert if I'm feeling like something sweet. I know what will make me feel good physically and mentally. I still struggle with finding the perfect eating balance, but life is a journey, not a destination, so it isn't perfection—even though I constantly strive for it.

Full disclosure: This is one of my struggles—I am hard on myself! I have high expectations! I'm still working through giving myself a break, and I'm over fifty! I'm never satisfied with where my physical self is at, and I think that has to do in part with what has kept me going. It's also a way of life. Jonn and I laugh because when we used to go on a weekend getaway, we'd pack junk food and treats. Now we arrange to go for hikes, on walks, and to places to work out. We golf, paddle board, bike ride, etc. So it's not all negative ☺. Don't get me wrong—we still have treats and junk food, just not like we used to!

TAKE TIME

to be still, reflect, listen, journal, and pray.

How can you maintain balance in your life and support your energy to manage health and responsibilities effectively?

_____

_____

_____

_____

_____

_____

_____

_____

_____

_____

_____

_____

_____
_____
_____
_____
_____
_____
_____
_____
_____
_____
_____
_____
_____

PRAY

Lord, help me to know
that you love me just as I
am—when I am balanced
and when I'm not! Amen!

MENTAL WELLNESS
Love Is Fuel for the Soul!

"Love is patient, love is
kind. It does not envy, it
does not boast, it is not
proud. It does not dishonor
others, it is not self-seeking,
it is not easily angered, it
keeps no record of wrongs"
(1 Corinthians 13:4–5).

Love yourself! Be patient with yourself! Be kind to yourself! My mom used to always tell me this as a kid, and I didn't understand it. I thought, *Well, that's self-centred!* But I get it now! Thanks, Mom!

Trust me, when you love yourself and work on your self-care and get your validation not from other people but from God and your own thoughts, you can be the best person for those around you. When your mental and physical wellness are your priority, you'll have confidence to be the best version of yourself—the best partner, the best parent, the best co-worker, the best boss, the best friend, the best sister/brother, daughter/son, etc. If you love who you are, you can give love and have understanding, essentially being healthy all around! This doesn't mean you need to be perfect. Mental and physical wellness is a journey to travel through, an adventure to experience, a trail to discover, a road to navigate. It's not one destination or final finish line. There are many destinations and finish lines along the way.

> "Remember, you are braver than you believe, stronger than you seem, and smarter than you think!"
> —Christopher Robin[7]

YOU MUST TAKE CARE OF YOUR MIND!

You might have a diagnosed mental health issue due to a chemical imbalance and/or other medical related reasons, but if it's undiagnosed and you know you don't feel right,

---

[7] From the movie Pooh's Gran Adventure: The Search for Christopher Robin (1997), Walt Disney Home Entertainment.

please seek help! There are many ways to seek help, such as talking to a coach, counsellor, pastor, help lines, doctors, nurses' line, friends, co-workers, teacher, parents, brother, sister, grandparent, aunt, uncle. The point is, reach-out. Do not stay silent! You are not alone, and you don't need to suffer in silence! Resources are out there, and many people can lead you to them. If at first you don't succeed, try and try again. This is called our life's journey. Don't give up!

TAKE TIME
to be still, reflect, listen, journal, and pray.

What can you do to prioritize self-love in your life, and
how do you believe this will positively impact your relationships and overall well-being?

_____

_____

_____

_____

_____

_____

_____

_____

_____

_____

_____

_____

_____

_____

_____

_____

_____

_____

_____

_____

PRAY

Dear Lord, thank you
for loving me. Let me see
what you see. Give me
your lens. Show me how
to love myself through
my thoughts just as you
created me and love me.
Amen.

HABITS: THE GOOD, THE BAD, THE UGLY

Don't Get Stuck in a Pothole!

"He lifted me out of the
slimy pit, out of the mud
and mire; he set my feet on
a rock and gave me a firm
place to stand."
(Psalm 40:2)

Are you looking to change a habit that's not serving you? First you need a road map, which is your plan and strategy. Like most things in life, this will give you the best chance at success. Write it down! Write it down every day! Let me be clear here—I'm not talking about addiction. There's a big difference between a habit that's not serving you and addiction.

> "You are not supposed to
> be the same person you
> were a year, month, day or
> even five seconds ago. You
> were designed to grow.
> —Mel Robbins[8]

Another full disclosure: I am an addict. My drug of choice is nicotine. I have to continuously battle against this in my life. I lean on Jesus. I give my shame and my weakness to God. I'm not perfect; I too have flaws. Because I am flawed, I need Jesus, so I pray for the chains of addiction to be broken. I pray for grace, strength, love, peace, and forgiveness. And then I forgive myself! I love myself! I see that God made me who I am, and I am loved!

WIKIPEDIA DEFINITIONS

A habit is routine of behaviour that is repeated regularly and tends to occur subconsciously.[9]

Addiction is generally a neuropsychological disorder defining pervasive and intense urge to engage in maladap-

---

[8] "27 Mel Robbins Quotes for Inspiration in Life," Inspire Your Success, accessed November 18, 2024, https://www.inspireyoursuccess.com/mel-robbins-quotes/.

[9] "Habit," Wikipedia, last modified October 9, 2024, https://en.wikipedia.org/wiki/Habit.

tive behaviours providing immediate sensory rewards, despite their harmful consequences.[10]

Making a lifestyle change?

Want to rid yourself of a bad habit?

Create a healthy habit?

You have the ability to change any type of habit you want! The key word here is *want*!

You are capable! You are strong!

"God is our refuge and strength, an ever-present help in trouble" (Psalm 46:1).

When I think of bad habits or poor behaviours, or anything that no longer serves me in a positive or healthy way, I try to understand why by breaking it apart. Why am I doing this? How is it serving me mentally and physically? What are the different levels of this bad habit? How can I change a few of the key components? How can I change the negative belief system I've associated with this? I remind myself why this isn't good for me any longer, over and over and over, until I believe it!

The next step is to have a plan and strategy for success, something that helps you when the habit or its trigger arises. I think of all the things that help me break it. For ease of understanding, let's continue calling it a bad

---

[10] "Addiction," Wikipedia, last modified October 22, 2024, https://en.wikipedia.org/wiki/Addiction.

habit. I really prefer to use "behaviours that no longer serve me."

"*He gives strength to the weary, and to him who has no might He increases power*" (Isaiah 40:29, AMP).

I've done research on the break-down of how a habit, good or bad, is created. A habit is a small decision you make to perform an action. It's a ritual or behaviour that becomes automatic, so you don't have to think about it. James Clear wrote the book *Atomic Habits*. He explains that habits run through four stages in the same order. Makes sense to me. Learning these stages helps to break down a habit.

Four stages to a habit: *CUE – CRAVING – RESPONSE – REWARD*

James writes that making tiny changes make a big difference. This is essentially what I did when I changed my lifestyle to healthier living. He talks about putting systems into place. You have a goal, but to get there you need a system in place. James uses this example, which I love, because I can truly relate to it with two-and-a-half of my children. (I say two-and-a-half because it's two for sure and one half the time—you know who you are). If your goal is to have a clean room and you gather motivation to clean it but you don't change the habit of never putting anything away, you will once again have a messy room and have to gather your motivation to clean it. Or you can change your habit of being slobbish, and then your goal of having a clean room will always be easy to achieve.

> "Achieving a goal only
> changes your life for the
> moment."[11]
> —James Clear

This is so true. I definitely recommend this book to get the full idea!

Side Note: Book recommendation—The Bible! You won't regret it!

I've had a goal of finishing this book for several years. I've been working on and off on it and always ended up feeling overwhelmed because I had focused on the goal of finishing it and not a system to complete it. Now I have a system. Thank you, God, Becky Keen, and James Clear!

> "Small things are not small at
> all. They are the most important
> things of all. And they add up."[12]
> —Mel Robbins

---

[11] James Clear, Atomic Habits: An Easy & Proven Way to Build Good Habits & Break Bad Ones (New York, NY: Avery Publishing, 2018), 25.
[12] "Top 80 Mel Robbins Quotes," Quotefancy, accessed November 1, 2024, https://quotefancy.com/mel-robbins-quotes.

TAKE TIME
to be still, reflect, listen, journal, and pray.

What habits are you currently trying to change or improve in your life? What strategies do you have in place to support your journey toward positive transformation? What's helping and what is not? Is there something you can pick up and/or something you can let go of?

_____

_____

_____

_____

_____

_____

_____

_____

_____

_____

_____

_____

_____

_____

_____

_____

_____

_____

_____

PRAY

Jesus, help me to break
the chains of the habits
that are not serving me
but are weighing me
down. Give me your
strength to do my part in
the hard work that it takes
to be free. Please carry
me when it becomes too
much. Amen!

CHOOSE GRATITUDE
Every Mile Is a Blessing!

"In every situation [no matter what the circumstances] be thankful and continually give thanks to God; for this is the will of God for you in Christ Jesus"
(1 Thessalonians 5:18, AMP).

Gratitude is a powerful tool that gives you the ability to change your focus in, or about, your life. Gratitude leans, directs, pushes, and catapults you toward a positive path, toward things that are good emotionally and physically and toward achievements, little or big. It helps you to appreciate the little things that you may be taking for granted.

Gratitude plug! I am so grateful to my husband, Jonn, for his encouragement, love, editing, prayers, and support with this book. I'm more in love with you today than yesterday. How is this even possible?

> "At times our own light goes out and is rekindled by a spark from another person. Each of us has cause to think with deep gratitude of those who have lighted the flame within us.
> —Albert Schweitzer[13]

I am so grateful for family and friends who have loved and supported me on my journey.

> "Everything we do should be a result of our gratitude for what God has done for us."
> —Lauryn Hill[14]

---

[13] Albert Schweitzer Quotes, BrainyQuote, accessed November 12, 2024, https://www.brainyquote.com/quotes/albert_schweitzer_402282.
[14] Lauryn Hill Quotes, BrainyQuote, accessed November 12, 2024, https://www.brainyquote.com/quotes/lauryn_hill_328378.

Did you know that gratitude and anxiety can't exist in the brain at the same time? You can't feel anxious while feeling gratitude. How incredible is it that God tells us in Philippians 4:6–7 to not be anxious for anything but in everything by prayer and petition be thankful! Wow! Just shows how God created us and is completely in line with science.

Two of my best friends keep gratitude journals. I've used this throughout my life at various times, usually when I need to tap back into a healthy path, when things feel like they're overwhelming or out of control, and when my anxiety is at a peak. This gives great perspective. When keeping a gratitude journal, I'm often grateful for the same things daily. I've consistently been writing in a gratitude and prayer journal for a while now, so, I can speak to the benefits of this!

GRATITUDE BREAK: WHAT ARE YOU GRATEFUL FOR?

Take a moment to appreciate these things in your life:

One person I am grateful for is _____, because _____.

A situation I am grateful for is _____, because _____.

A moment I am grateful for is _____,
because _____.

An experience I am grateful for is _____,
because _____.

What did you notice while doing this exercise. Did you feel a shift physically or emotionally? Notice what changed in your body and mind. Did you physically move? Did your body relax? Do you feel more or less comfortable? Do you feel joy, peace, love, or something completely different? Just sit with it.

If you've always wanted to engage in a gratitude journal but never got started, here's a helpful strategy. Pick up a journal, or create one on your laptop or phone if that appeals to you. Set a reminder in your calendar with a designated time that works for you to write (morning, afternoon, evening).

The idea is to write in it every day. Start with one thing that you're grateful for and build on that each day. This can be anything you appreciate, from menial to meaningful. As you get into it, you can add the reasoning behind your gratitude. Have fun with it!

I believe it's a fantastic tool! What are you struggling with? Journaling can help you to get past something you're stuck on, like a negative action or thought, an unproductive path, an unhealthy, troubled, or un-empowered relationship of any kind, intimate or not, an uninspiring job, and so on. Writing in a gratitude journal is beneficial to your healing process and gives you guidance and the ability to move forward in a positive direction. It also allows you to accept things that aren't in your control. You only have control over what you do and how you react! *Change your focus! It's a choice!*

It's also a good practice to share your gratitude at the dinner table with kids, parents, friends, and siblings. We did this as a family. Highs and lows! My kids loved it. It's a great tool to find out where the people in your life are at and how they're coping, as things will pop up. It creates conversations you may not otherwise have. Thank you, Jennifer Kathleen, again! She's full of great ideas, great practices, and great tools! Both my husband and I write in a daily gratitude and prayer journal in the morning. This helps get me in the right frame of mind for my day ahead.

Some days, just being grateful that I have a bed to sleep in when it's cold outside and that I woke up to conquer the day is enough to start my day in a grateful direction. Changing your perspective helps you see the things that are beautiful, which helps you to appreciate what's around you. Everyone can find one thing.

"I am happy because I am grateful. I choose to be grateful. That allows me to be happy."[15]
—Will Arnett

Did you know that depending on the version you're reading, the Bible mentions the word "gratitude" 157 times? Wow! Other versions may use the term "thanks" or "thanksgiving."

You do have a choice. I'm not saying that the choice will always be easy! Take a leap! This is your life journey of learning and growing prior to eternity. You can choose to be miserable in your life and/or circumstances, which leads to self-pity and feeling like a victim, or you can choose to find gratitude, which ultimately leads to joy and happiness regardless of what's going on in your life. Gratitude is a rock-solid foundational practice. The more you put into it, the stronger your foundation becomes and the less you'll be affected by your circumstances.

"Some people could be given an entire field of roses and only see the thorns in it.

---

[15] "Will Arnett Quotes," BrainyQuotes, accessed November 1, 2024, https://www.brainyquote.com/quotes/will_arnett_801179.

> Others could be given
> a single weed and only see
> the wildflower in it.
> Perception is a key
> component to gratitude.
> And gratitude is a key
> component to joy."[16]
> —Amy Weatherby

What do you want to focus on? What will be the foundation of your life—rock or sand?

> Therefore everyone who
> hears these words of mine
> and puts them into prac-
> tice is like a wise man
> who built his house on
> rock. The rain came down,
> the streams rose, and
> the winds blew and beat
> against that house; yet it
> did not fall, because it had

---

[16] Church of St. John the Evangelist Parish Newsletter, accessed November 1, 2024, https://kilbarrackfoxfieldparish.ie/church-of-st-john-the-evangelist-kilbarrack-foxfield-parish-newsletter-sunday-22nd-august-2021-twenty-first-sunday-in-ordinary-time/.

its foundation on the rock. But everyone who hears these words of mine and does not put them into practice is like a foolish man who built his house on sand. The rain came down, the stream rose, and the winds blew and beat down against that house, and it fell with a great crash. (Matthew 7:24–27)

TAKE TIME

to be still, reflect, listen, journal, and pray.

How can you incorporate gratitude into your daily routine? What steps can you take to create a habit? Do you believe this practice will positively impact your overall well-being and perspective?

_____

_____

_____

_____

_____

_____

_____

_____

_____

_____

_____

_____

_____

_____

_____

_____

PRAY

Lord, please give me
a heart filled with
gratitude. Fill my mind
with a positive, grateful
perspective. Help me to
capture, let go of, and cast
out negative thoughts that
lead to self-pity. Thank
you for blessing me with
the people you have
placed in my life—the
people who help me to
learn and grow and who
make me a better person!
Amen!

ANXIETY

A smooth ride never made for a skillful driver!

Consider it pure joy, my brothers and sisters, whenever you face trials of many kinds, because you know that the testing of your faith produces perseverance. Let perseverance finish its work so that you may be mature and complete, not lacking anything. (James 1:2–4)

According to the American Psychiatric Association, anxiety is a normal reaction to stress. It's the anticipation of a future concern. Mild anxiety can be a good thing and can alert us to dangers. Fear becomes the emotional response that triggers the fight or flight reaction. Panic attacks become the physical and psychological reaction and can cause some or all of these symptoms: rapid heart rate, sweating, shaking, shortness of breath, chest pains, dizziness, a choking feeling, numbness or tingling, chills or hot flashes, nausea, fear of losing control, fear of dying.

> For God did not give us a spirit of timidity or cowardice or fear, but [He has given us a spirit] of power and of love sound judgment and personal discipline [abilities that result in a calm, well-balanced mind and self-control].
> (2 Timothy 1:7, AMP)

My panic attacks came on from being overwhelmed and stressed, feeling like things were unmanageable. I felt uncomfortable, unsafe, and not in control. I had these panic attacks most of my life—as a child, through my teen years, and as a young adult. I called them "Nervous Bum" before I knew what a panic attack was. This is actually a thing! Who knew?

In an article written by Elizabeth Harris, the author explains that high stress can affect your digestive system. She calls it "Anxiety Poops." She quotes a clinical and holistic nutritionist who describes how stress and anxiety increase hormones such as cortisol, adrenaline, and serotonin, which affects your digestive system by creating nervous bum or anxiety poops. "Serotonin is a neurotransmitter and a hormone involved in the peristaltic reflex (moving food thru the gastrointestinal tract) During heighted anxiety, the amount of serotonin increases in your gut and can cause spasms to happen throughout your entire colon."[17] These spasms can induce unexpected BMs.

Funny side note: Years ago, my husband had never heard the term "BM," so he said, "What does that stand for—big massive?" It still makes me giggle! I am now editing and still laughing.

As much as I've gotten a good handle on how to deal with my anxiety, sometimes the combo of stress, discomfort, nervousness, and hormones are all too much, and the very unwelcomed nervous bum hits me! Ahhhhh! That's me—horrified! This has happened countless times

---

[17] Maya Eid, "Anxiety Poop: Why It Happens and How to Treat," Healthline, March 10, 2021, https://www.healthline.com/health/mental-health/is-anxiety-making-you-poop-heres-how-to-soothe.

throughout my life. It happened to me while I was waiting in a line that was getting longer and longer, with nowhere to go and no chance to leave. I was waiting for my first COVID vaccine shot! I had one of the first appointments of the day, and the vaccines were late to arrive at the immunization site. I was already nervous about the entire situation and process. The moment the line started to move, my discomfort subsided, which released my protective nervous system and I felt completely and totally fine! No bathroom required!

It wasn't until after I had experienced a major panic attack at a friend's baby shower when I was thirty-one years old that a doctor told me I had experienced a panic attack. He prescribed Ativan, which ironically made my anxiety hit the all-time peak! This didn't fix the problem. It only made me drowsy and feel out of control again. It was then that I realized I'd had panic attacks my entire life, whenever I'd felt uncomfortable or that something wasn't in my or my caregiver's control. I was having panic attacks when I didn't feel safe, or like I was responsible for everyone and everything. Basically overwhelmed!

I have worked through this with my coach, Becky Keen. I learned to look at these reactions and notice what's happening in my body without attaching anything to it or trying to fix it or wish it away. How do you feel physically? My heart is racing. My chest feels tight; I feel nauseous. Don't attach any negative thoughts to this; just do a full physical body scan. Ask yourself, "What is my body telling me?"

"Your nervous system is so smart and wise!" Becky would say. Thank you, Becky! This reaction is my nervous system being wise! Of course, it's how we were created. It's protecting me from feeling unsafe. Notice and sit with it and just be okay with not being okay. This is so powerful! I have lived it and put it into practice! It works! Try it!

I see now that experiencing panic attacks and extreme anxiety helped me to focus on what matters and to let go of what doesn't matter. This doesn't mean that I now sail through life without a care or worry in the world. Not a true story! I still have to work through these feelings as they come up or things change around me, but I approach it differently. I pray. I lean on God for wisdom through reading His Word. I listen to God. I pray some more. I listen to sermons. I sit with all of it. I tell myself it's okay to not be okay! I ask myself what am I protecting myself from. I validate my feelings and know my body is wise and fearfully and wonderfully made! I give myself space and time to slow down. I give myself permission to say no. I never used to! God doesn't want you to be fearful.

"*I sought the Lord [on the authority if His word], and He answered me, and delivered me from all my fears*" (Psalm 34:4, AMP). Even if you don't have panic attacks or suffer from anxiety, this truth helps with any type of stress, worry, or fear. It will help you quit something and change a habit that's not serving you and/or is controlling you and creating a negative response in your body and mind.

Learning to breathe and being active is another valued tool for me! I wish I'd found breath work at a younger age, or realized the benefits of using my physical body work to complement my mental health. Thank you, Christie, bestie for life, for always encouraging me, never giving up on me, and reminding me to breathe!

Let's stop here for a moment to do a breathing exercise. You're likely already in a comfortable seated or lying down position, since you're reading. If you're listening to the audio book in the car, then please don't close your eyes. Just kidding, I don't think this will be an audio book. Wait! Was that a limiting belief!? I think it was!

Box Breathing helps to regulate and reset your breath and nervous system. It also reduces stress and anxiety.

Imagine a box shape. Inhale for two to five counts, thinking about travelling up one side of the box, then hold your breath for two to five counts while imagining you're travelling along the top of the box, then exhale for two to five counts travelling down the other side of the box, then hold your breath for two to five counts along the bottom of the box. Then repeat. I use four counts, so I would inhale for four counts, hold for four counts, exhale for four counts, and hold again for four counts. You can adjust the counts to what works in your body. Just make sure that they're equal counts for the inhale, hold, and exhale. Repeat this box pattern for as long as you like. Five to ten times is a great guideline, but do what works for you. Close your eyes if that's comfortable for you, or relax your eyes into a soft stare and begin.

How do you feel? Notice what you're feeling in your body. Start with your head, shoulders, chest, arms, hands, stomach, hips, legs, and feet. You can do this anywhere, anytime. I have and I do!

Don't have time for Box Breathing? A quick breathing technique would be to constrict your throat slightly so that when you inhale and exhale, your breath is audible to you. With your mouth closed, inhale slowly through your nose, hold for just one count, then slowly exhale, either through your nose or mouth. Hold this for one and repeat ten times, or for as long or as little as you need.

I have definitely had times when my anxiety was in peaks and valleys. In 2001, when I realized what it really was, I listened to tape cassettes that my stepdad, Geoff, gave me about managing anxiety, as he had dealt with it too. I would walk and listen to this woman who talked about reframing your thoughts and mind, only she didn't call it that. This did help, much more than the Ativan, but it was always in the back of my mind and would creep in unexpectantly, so I changed my life to manage it.

God called us back to church during Christmas dinner at my dad and stepmom's house in 2002. Renee, my stepmom, was bold and stepped out for Christ. She said it like it is: we are called to be in community with each other. She was right, even though at the time I argued that you didn't need to be in church to have a relationship with Jesus. And really you don't, but my relationship with Jesus was weak, maybe even non-existent, because I wasn't attending church. I wasn't reading the Bible or growing in my faith.

One of God's Ten Commandments is to keep the seventh day a holy Sabbath day. One of the ways we follow this commandment is by worshipping and giving thanks to God.

Believers strengthen each other through being in community together (church) and by building relationships through sharing our faith and experiences, and by supporting and praying together and for each other: "*For where two or three gather in my name, there am I with them*" (Matthew 18:20).

My husband, my toddler, my career, my family, and my friends all took top priority. I didn't feel like I had space for church. Regardless, God had other plans, and we went! We created the space, and I wouldn't change it for anything, ever! As we do, Jonn and I dove in with two feet. We loved going to church, and our daughter loved going to church. I felt safe, warm, and loved. I felt like I was home. And it's not like I didn't feel loved before, but this was a different kind of love. At the time, we told the pastor that everyone we knew was going to come, and the church would be filled, because everyone needs the love of Jesus in their lives.

We were surrounded by a community that offered acceptance, love, and support. We joined a small group. Later, as we were driving home from this small group, we realized that it was actually a Bible study! We laughed hysterically on our drive home—we, Jonn and Simone, were attending a Bible study! We'd always thought there was a stigma attached to this. We'd also judged that church, but we found out how wrong we were. Again, God's plan! Absolutely amazing! We eventually hosted groups, and my husband joined the worship team; our kids were part of the youth group and kids' program. I joined the women's group. We loved every single minute of it. The good, the bad, and the ugly! It was then that I made the decision to get baptized. I was renewed! I felt so loved! I was completely fulfilled!

While we were attending church, I still had bouts of anxiety. This is where I learned to cast my fear onto God. He wants to take your worries and fears from you. This took my anxiety away from me for years. I would have the thought, and then the anxiety would come along with a nervous system reaction. I started to give that thought to God. I would imagine sitting on His lap, like a grandfather and his grandchild. I would pray, "God, give me your peace and calm," and I would feel it wash over me. Thank you, Holy Spirit! This gave me safety, warmth, and comfort. I felt His love. Anxiety is a whisper from the devil! So it was amazing to feel His peace. I cast my fears/worries on to Him over and over, until the anxiety left me completely. What a wonderful promise from God to be able to just give it to Him.

Being an only child, I wanted a big family, as I came from a huge extended family. I had married the man of my dreams, and all I wanted was to have his children and be his partner. We had trouble conceiving each of our children. God gave us our first little miracle in 1999. Our conceiving journey lasted twelve years. We had many miscarriages, including two ectopic pregnancies with a couple of life-threatening emergency surgeries. Our small group supported us and prayed, and thus our second child, through IVF, was born. And then our miracle number three, also through IVF, was born during these years walking with God.

Lots of things happened in that part of our journey at the church, including a couple of church splits that resulted in church hurt for many. I won't go into it. Again, people aren't perfect, and church isn't perfect because of that. Around 2013/2014, we stopped attending church due to many factors, mainly because life got busy with three kids in various activities, and our own career choices. This was a big mistake on our part, and we completely regret it! But don't worry, because God called us back again!

TAKE TIME
to be still, reflect, listen, journal, and pray.

What actions can you take to support your mental and emotional well-being? Would you use any of the strategies I have mentioned? Which ones resonate with you? What are some others that would work for you?

_____

_____

_____

_____

_____

_____

_____

_____

_____

_____

_____

_____

_____

_____

_____

_____

_____

_____

_____

_____

PRAY

Thank you, Lord, that
you don't give us a spirit
of fear. Thank you that
you tell us in your Word,
over and over, not to be
afraid, that you are with
us always. Help me to let
go of my fears, capture
my thoughts, and cast it
all to you. Amen!

CHOOSE TO BE THE LEADER OF YOUR LIFE

Pave Your Way!

*"Each one should test
their own actions. Then
they can take pride in
themselves alone, without
comparing themselves to
someone else, for each one
should carry their own
load"* (Galatians 6:4–5).

No one can be a leader in all things. We all have strengths in different areas. How would this world function if everyone was the same? Not everyone can be a great bowler! Well, I suppose everyone could be a great bowler if they put in the hours and effort and training and visualizing required, even if they weren't a naturally talented bowler! LOL!

This is why diversity is a beautiful thing! Be proud of who you are! You are a leader, because you are first and foremost the leader and controller of your life, your focus, your reactions, your choices, your decisions, and your boundaries. You control what you allow in and what you project out. This is a lifelong practice, and I am still practising! Can you hear me telling this to my kids? I did, over and over!

Once you're aware of what mindful wellness looks like for you ...

Pause for side note: This doesn't mean perfection or that you won't have to continually work on it but will always be well. I became unwell early in 2023 due to many things and had to start my work again with God, with my husband, with my kids, with a couple of diehard supportive friends, with my parents, and with Becky. I had to be reminded of all the things I already knew and put them back into practice. It happens, and it's a journey!

... this gives you the ability to be the best leader you can be, whether it's of your own life or of others. It's okay not to be a leader in all things. This is why we're all different and we need to work together. Not everyone can or should lead.

Having said that, it's just as important to be a support person. Secretly, I believe effective support people often are the leaders but just not the face of the leader. They give the leaders the confidence, tools, and space to be leaders. I'm guessing you know which person I am. I'm a support through and through, which I believe in many situations makes me the leader. If you have the confidence in who you are, then you'll feel more fulfilled and have less of a need to be something that you're not! You can be okay with who you are and own it! Be proud of your role and purpose. You are needed and important.

"*If the whole body were an eye, where would the hearing be? If the whole [body] were an ear, where would be the sense of smell be?*" (1 Corinthians 12:17, AMP). I feel disheartened when people say, "I am just this." For example, a colleague of mine used to say to clients, "I can't answer that because I'm just the secretary." My answer to that is that you're not just the secretary—you are the secretary, and you're darn good at being the secretary. Without you, the "professionals" wouldn't be able to run their business. You give them space and a foundation to fulfill client needs, because you deal with the things they can't and you give them the support they need to complete the process! Reframe your words and thoughts!

I'm the office manager at my mom's CPA firm. She has said many times that without my support, she couldn't run a successful business. The words of a great leader appreciate and give credit where credit is due! She is the face and the leader of our company, and she recognizes that the support team has helped make her a great leader. I've spent my life working with my mom, and there have been challenges for sure as I, the boss' daughter, managed an office of mostly women personnel and tried to earn the respect of the staff who watched me grow into my role over the years. But we are a great team. I have truly loved it and sometimes disliked it, but ultimately, I learned so much working for her. I am so grateful and have appreciated this time with my mom. I wouldn't have wanted to work for anyone else. This experience has been a part of shaping who I am.

> But now [as things really are], God has placed and arranged the parts in the body, each one of them, just as He willed and saw fit [with the best balance of function]. If they all were one single organ, where would [the rest of] the body be? But now [as things really are] there

> are many parts [different
> limbs and organs], but a
> single body. The eye can-
> not say to the hand, "I
> have no need for you,"
> nor again the head to the
> feet, I have no need for
> you." (1 Corinthians 12:18–
> 21, AMP)

God gives us spiritual gifts, and we need each other to function like a healthy body. No one part or gift is better or more important than the other. This is good stuff. I encourage you to read the entire chapter. It just makes so much sense.

Putting the Word to Work

Do you ever struggle with your role, thinking others are called to more important work? In Nehemiah 3:26-31, some workers were called to repair large portions of the wall, while others were to repair

> only the section in front
> of their own house. Be en-
> couraged: All work done
> for God is significant; and
> the most important thing
> is to be obedient to do
> what God calls you to do.[18]
> —Joyce Meyer

Behind every great leader is an amazing team! And every great leader knows that it's because of their team that is working with them that they can be great! A pro athlete, for example, begins with parents, coaches, and a willing, determined child. They are dedicated to the schedule at a young age. Parents enroll and transport them to extra classes or training. They receive guidance and help from coaches and mentors, training specialists, personal assistants, nutritionists, managers, partners, and content creators. Think about all the people and support it takes to get them where they are. If you're a professional athlete, that's fantastic. You have dedicated your life to working hard toward your goals and dreams, and you also know exactly what I'm talking about!

---

[18] The Every Day Life Bible (New York, NY: Warner Faith, 2006), 731.

When I speak of leadership, I truly mean in all aspects of life, not just the obvious roles in the workplace. The most successful of these have the best support people in place. But leaders are also in your home: men, fathers, single mothers, grandparents, and other family members. There are leaders in friendship and mentorship who show kindness and compassion.

> "Empowering those around you to be heard and valued makes the difference between a leader who simply instructs and one who inspires."[19]
> —Adena Friedman, Nasdaq CEO

---

[19] "Adena Friedman Quotes," BrainyQuote, accessed November 1, 2024, https://www.brainyquote.com/quotes/adena_friedman_847834.

TAKE TIME
to be still, reflect, listen, journal, and pray.

In what areas of your life do you feel you could improve
your leadership? Do you see yourself more as a leader or a
supporter? How might you shift toward the other role to
achieve a better balance in your life?

_____

_____

_____

_____

_____

_____

_____

_____

_____

_____

_____

_____

_____

_____

_____

_____

_____

_____

PRAY

God, help me to be
inspiring and uplifting to
those around me. Help
me to be your light of
love and encouragement.
Help me to see the value
of my role and purpose.
Guide me to be the leader
of my life. Amen!

CHOOSE CONFIDENCE OVER ARROGANCE

Let Your Motoring Skills Speak for Themselves!

Do nothing from selfishness or empty conceit [through factional motives, or strife], but with [an attitude of] humility [being neither arrogant nor self-righteous], regard others as more important than yourselves. Do not merely look out for your own personal interests, but also for the interests of others. (Philippians 2:3–4, AMP)

BEING HUMBLE IS SO ATTRACTIVE!

Humble: having or showing a modest or low estimate of one's own importance.[20]

But the benefits of humility do not extend to just our leaders. Nascent research suggests that this lovely quality is good for us individually and for our relationships. For example, humble people handle stress more effectively and report higher levels of physical and mental well-being. They also show greater generosity, helpfulness, and gratitude-all things that can only serve to draw us closer to others.[21]

---

[20] Oxford English Dictionary, s.v. "humble," accessed November 12, 2024, https://www.oed.com/search/dictionary/?q=humble&tl=true.

[21] Vicki Zakrzewski, "How Humility Will Make You the Greatest Person Ever," Greater Good Magazine, January 12, 2016, https://greatergood.berkeley.edu/article/item/humility_will_make_you_greatest_person_ever

There's a big difference here! Announcing your greatness is behaving arrogantly and pridefully! Someone who exudes confidence doesn't need to tell everyone about it! If your confidence requires you to make everyone around you aware of it, then you're not exuding self-confidence—you're acting self-consciously. If you require your confidence to be validated, then you're not confident. Let your actions, compassion, and reactions show your confidence! It's not attractive when a person needs to make others feel less than them to feel empowered. I believe that most people who do this aren't aware of it. These are people who constantly talk about themselves and always take the credit for ideas, even if they didn't come from them. They need constant approval to be built up.

Confident people show it through actions. They don't need the outside validation, and it's louder than words. It is 100 per cent a self-confidence issue. There's a difference between promoting yourself and needing approval. The goal is not to make the people around you feel badly and for everyone to like you, but it's for personal fulfillment, so that you can be the best version of yourself. The more you love, accept, and embrace who you are, the more confidence you'll have. The more you love, accept, and embrace the people around you, the more your confidence will shine through: "*Blessed are the meek, for they will inherit the earth*" (Matthew 5:5).

TAKE TIME
to be still, reflect, listen, journal, and pray.

What practices can you adopt to navigate the fine line
between confidence and arrogance while still remaining
humble?

_____

_____

_____

_____

_____

_____

_____

_____

_____

_____

_____

_____

_____

_____

_____

_____

_____

_____

_____

_____

_____

PRAY

Lord, please give me
the wisdom to know
the difference between
confidence and arrogance,
and guide me to have a
humble heart! Amen!

CHOOSE KINDNESS!
Drive with Courtesy, Arrive with Respect!

I am giving you a commandment, that you love one another. Just as I have loved you, so you too are to love one another. By this everyone will know that you are My disciples, if you have love and unselfish concern for one another.
(John 13:34–35, AMP)

There are so many Bible verses on love and kindness. I don't even know what else to say. I mean, God really says it all! He commands us to love one another as He loves us! He loves us so much that He gave His one and only Son! It's not complicated. We can't fathom God's love for us! He loves us as we love our own children. If we just love and show kindness to one another to the capacity that we've been given, what a different world this would be.

Kindness is a fruit of the Spirit, and niceness is of the flesh and people-pleasing. The difference between being kind and being nice is that when you are kind, you're doing so at the sacrifice of your own needs and desires.[22]

Kindness doesn't cost anything. The value of the gain is worth more to you, and to the recipient it can be day-to-night life-changing.

This all ties in together with your choices of your reactions. You are in control of you and what you choose.

> So, as God's own chosen people, who are holy [set apart, sanctified for His purpose] and well-beloved [by God Himself], put on a heart of compassion, kindness, humility, gentleness, and patience [which

[22] Withtheperrys (@WithThePerrys). Instagram post. October 25, 2024. https://www.instagram.com/reel/DBjPRHzuul3/?igsh=MXM4eTRndnR-vamQ4ZQ%3D%3D.

> has the power to endure
> whatever injustice or un-
> pleasantness comes, with
> good temper].
> (Colossians 3:12, AMP)

When are we going to become "Team Human Race?" Let's work together! Competition has value and is a healthy practice.

At the end of the day, don't we all want the same thing? To have purpose and fulfillment? To feel love and joy on earth? To live and gain experiences and memories to take with us? To build generational legacies, businesses, and solutions and to be better personally and collectively? To be competitive through integrity? Ultimately, we want to spend eternity feeling God's love and joy, which we can't even understand or describe on earth.

> with all humility [forsak-
> ing self-righteousness],
> and gentleness [maintain-
> ing self-control], with pa-
> tience, bearing with one
> another in [unselfish] love.
> Make every effort to keep

the oneness of the Spirit
in the bond of peace [each
individual working to-
gether to make the whole
successful].
(Ephesians 4:2–3, AMP)

I find this interesting. Why do some politicians in a political race act like poorly behaved children who were never taught not to call names or bully others? I would never vote for someone who built their campaign on all the wrong the opposition have done in the past. I would like to hear your opinions, goals, and aspirations for our community or country without putting someone else down or slandering them. I can hear your valid points without that sort of tactic.

I believe that Canadians are smart people and that the political parties would be surprised at how many people are capable of hearing their plan for our country rather than spewing off misgivings about other parties. I understand that it's important to know when someone has done a poor job of leading or fulfilling their civic duty, but there are different ways to do this. I have never understood this type of advocating for oneself, and not just with politicians. Imagine if everyone chose kindness and promoted or advocated for themselves through what they are willing to do and how they would implement it. Simply give the people your agenda and how you propose to get it done, and evidence of truth behind your ability to get it done. Let's use that soapbox to promote through positive energy.

What a different world if we could get rid of hate. I hate that word "hate!" Shudder! I only use this word to make someone understand the deep, dark feeling I have about what I am talking about. I actually *hate* raw butter!

TAKE TIME
to be still, reflect, listen, journal, and pray.

What does kindness mean to you? In what situations do
you find it challenging to cultivate kindness? How can
you change this?

_____

_____

_____

_____

_____

_____

_____

_____

_____

_____

_____

_____

_____

_____

_____

_____

_____

_____

_____

_____

_____

PRAY

Thank you that you love
us, Lord. Clear my heart,
mind, and soul of hatred,
Jesus, from the smallest
form of it to the biggest. I
ask the Holy Spirit to give
me a spirit of kindness so
I can love as you love us.
Amen!

CHOOSE FORGIVENESS
Letting Go of Road Rage!

"bearing graciously with
one another, and willing
forgiving each other if one
has cause for complaint
against another; just as the
Lord has forgiven you, so
should you forgive."
(Colossians 3:13, AMP)

Choose forgiveness for yourself first and foremost! Why? you ask. Because anger and hatred can fester and grow into a darkness that will mainly affect you! Do this as part of self-love, self-healing, self-kindness for you! Don't hold on to anything that needs forgiving. I've had to forgive over and over, every day, until I truly felt it and believed it. And then I was free from the mental angst of that situation or conflict!

Forgiveness is a process, and you'll go through other feelings like hurt, anger, grief, and pain, but ultimately forgiveness will set you free! This is also true of forgiving yourself. Feel these feelings as they come up. Be aware of what's happening physically and mentally. Dealing with your mental and physical awareness will help you work toward forgiveness.

Today many people choose to cancel culture instead of forgive. I feel a genuine sadness for the people who have been cancelled; there's my compassionate heart bursting out again. I'm not talking about people who have no remorse or are repeat offenders. There are so many intricate situations. I could talk for hours on this subject. I'm talking about those people who are battling a past that they're trying to break free from, or who are trying to move forward from a mistake they made. Is there no recourse? Some people are born into a generational curse or poor parenting, which didn't give them a road map, but they want to do better. Are these people to be thrown out forever? Those who have asked for forgiveness but are met with isolation and shame.

The energy and effort required for the people cancelling others must be all-consuming and exhausting, ultimately harming themselves. I think some people believe they are setting good personal boundaries through cancelling someone and that they're justified. I suppose in some circumstances this is accurate. But in my own experience, if you've been cancelled, you know how incredibly lonely and mentally harmful it is. It can be devastating to be cut off from people, especially your own family or friends. It's the ultimate punishment and mental abuse. These days, youth do this to each other through social media platforms. They block and unadd each other. This is just another form of rejection on the internet playground that our kids are dealing with today, and it's a new form of mental warfare.

Do people find it easier to cancel, block, or unadd someone rather than finding forgiveness? What about working through the situation? How is this "cancel culture" serving society? How are people working through their stuff?

I'm curious. What does it say when people cancel someone? Are they saying that they live a perfect life with no mistakes? Is there no room for error and forgiveness anymore? Where is the line? How is the judgement determined? The line seems to be getting shorter, and in the end it all relates to hatred, and you know how I feel about that. This is opposite of what Jesus teaches. I know there are always exceptions or exceptional circumstances, but this type of resolve just seems to be more common today. Maybe it's just easier to walk away and not deal with people or teach people or learn and grow with each other. People are flawed. We make mistakes. People ruin good things. How can we be better together?

"*Then Peter came to Jesus and asked, 'Lord, how many times shall I forgive my brother and sister who sins against me? Up to seven times?' Jesus replied, I tell you, not seven times, but seventy-seven times*" (Matthew 18:21–22). The Lord's Prayer says, "*And forgive us our debts, as we have forgiven our debtors [letting go of both the wrong and the resentment]*" (Matthew 6:12, AMP).

Mother Teresa said:

> People are often unreasonable and
> self-centered.
> Forgive them anyway.
> If you are kind, people may ac-
> cuse you of ulterior motives.
> Be kind anyway.
> If you are honest, people may
> cheat.
> Be honest anyway.

If you find happiness, people may
be jealous.
Be happy anyway.
The good you do today may be
forgotten tomorrow.
Do good anyway.
Give the world the best you have,
and it may never be enough.
Give your best anyway.
For you see, in the end, it is be-
tween you and God. It was never
between you and them anyway.[23]

If you forgive someone, that doesn't mean you have
to be in their life. Just be kind and release the anger from
within. Work through your feelings. Learn and grow
yourself. Let's stop shaming and being critical of people! Once you forgive, let it go! To the people who have
been cancelled by people that they once cared for: Maybe
there's a reason you're not meant to travel this journey
with them. Sometimes God allows people to be removed
from our lives for a reason. Someday that reason will be
clear. Let them go!

---

[23] Author unknown. Based on the original poem by Kent Keith.

TAKE TIME

to be still, reflect, listen, journal, and pray.

Are you hanging on to unforgiveness? Are you looking
for forgiveness from someone? What does forgiveness
look like to you?

_____

_____

_____

_____

_____

_____

_____

_____

_____

_____

_____

_____

_____

_____

_____

_____

_____

_____

_____

_____

PRAY

Thank you for people like
Mother Teresa, who speak
words of truth, love, and
forgiveness, and through
whom your light shines.
Help me to soak up these
words, apply them to
my life, and grow into
the likeness of you—full
of love and forgiveness.
Amen!

BOUNDARIES AND BEHAVIOURS, PERSPECTIVE AND COMPASSION

Clear Parameters Lead to Safer Roads

> *"Let love be genuine. Abhor what is evil; hold fast to what is good. Love one another with brotherly affection. Outdo one another in showing honor."*
> (Romans 12:9–10, ESV)

BULLIES & MEANIES

S ometimes entertaining another perspective helps us understand where the behaviour is coming from, and then we can have compassion for people—even people who are unkind. But for your personal protection, create healthy boundaries. It's important! Most of the time when people are unkind, it isn't about you but more about themselves, their life, their experiences, their circumstances, their grief, their inability to deal with the pressures of life, or the absence of a relationship with God. Maybe they've never been given tools to work through their emotions. Maybe they choose to allow their circumstances to control their happiness. Maybe they rely on other people for their happiness. Maybe this has been going on from generation to generation.

I discovered through my own coaching that I am seriously affected by the happiness of the people around me. If my kids are unhappy, sad, or hurt, I feel it, big time. I'm working through this, feeling my feelings, and knowing that I can be happy even if they're not, because it doesn't make them happy for me to be unhappy.

Okay, hear me out on another thought. Can we teach emotional tools in school? Can mental preparedness be part of our school curriculum? I know we talk about right and wrong and treating each other kindly, but it's weak! Many parents and educators do teach these things to their kids in their care, but how amazing it would be if we made full courses on this subject from preschool to high school, teaching compassion, kindness, empathy, healthy boundaries, forgiveness, respectable communication skills, love, patience, humility, courage, determination, and compromise. How to live in and enjoy each moment by being present. Proper ways to use your breath to control physical body reactions. How to manifest the fruits of the Spirit. How to deal with the range of human emotions, from anger to joy.

Quick sidenote within the thought: Don't you just love a good podcast? Megan Fate Marshman—author, speaker, pastor—spoke at the "Combating Lies with Truth" girls conference and then talked about the event on the *Loving God, Loving People* podcast. At the conference, Megan would say, "I'm not enough," and the girls would reply with "Yes, that's a lie." But Megan says, "Here's the thing—that's not the lie. The lie is that you have to be."[24]

I feel like my mom really lived by this. She actually knew that she was enough always and never felt like she had to fit into anyone's definition of what is enough. I didn't inherit this from her at all! I never felt like anything I did was enough, so I love this because I don't even have to try to be.

Know that it's okay to feel your feelings! You don't need to escape your feelings but hit them head on. Learn about validating them and how to sit with them, and where to get help for depression or other mental health disorders. If we teach these things in school, maybe these disorders will

---

[24] Sun Valley Community Church, "Being Honest with Yourself and with God (with Megan Fate Marshman)," YouTube, March 12, 2024, 32:48, https://www.youtube.com/watch?v=bTvoL1OTSrU.

be discovered sooner, and all kids/teens can get the tools and assistance they need to manage before becoming an adult. Wow, what prepared adults we'd have!

The course could be expanded to include finance, budgeting, banking and money management, taxes, housing, and the cost of moving out on your own. Students would learn to give back and contribute to our society in a positive way, and how to be green and save our planet. Don't you think we could be so much happier if everyone knew the big secret that being happy is a choice? Everyone can be happy no matter what has happened in their life if they learn the tools to make that choice. Who wants to take the leap on this? I think it would be invaluable to our society.

I know what you're thinking: Isn't this the parents' job? You have a point, but some parents aren't equipped. And knowledge is power. It's as important as teaching our kids about the science of reproduction and awareness in that. How our bodies work physically *and* mentally is important to learn. If we had a base program in which everyone has the opportunity to learn these skills, they could learn these at school and get support at home as well. Many teachers spend a lot of time dealing with behaviour issues, so wouldn't it be great for them to have a structured, age-appropriate lesson, or professionally trained people come in and teach these skills? In my humble opinion, that would be amazing. I think some will say we already do this, but it depends on who you talk to.

Families can look very different with many different dynamics and situations. Some are out of the parents' control, and some are due to the choices made. I could name endless scenarios. Some kids are just raising themselves! Wouldn't it be amazing to have this program available to every child and really to get back to what's written in God's Word?

Having a relationship with Jesus, praying, and reading God's Word has given me much joy, peace, and comfort. My personal relationship has saved me from anxiety, fear, and worry! It has helped me forgive and be forgiven. If we were all a little more prepared for what adulthood was going to bring, maybe we would live in the moment and not be in such a rush to grow up. Actually, might be more of a "teen thing" (me) and maybe not so much a "child thing." I think children live in the moment, so we can learn this from them.

We can be quick to judge, criticize, or even cancel each other. I believe this is because we don't take that moment to consider what other people may be going through or what happened in their past or even their day. A little compassion goes a long way and will give you the ability to see the reasoning behind the behaviour. It really all ties together, doesn't it?

There is such a disconnect with texting, online platforms, and social media. It has created a wall that people can hide behind to say the things they shouldn't say. It allows people to be unkind, critical, and judgemental without any emotional attachment. You don't have control over other people's behaviour, only your reaction to it!

People who are unkind, bullying, or controlling of others are usually experiencing their own pain. Hurt people hurt people! They've learned this behaviour through the experience of being bullied or controlled themselves. This leads to being self-conscious and then needing to feel better about themselves by doing the same thing to others. Sometimes this is so no one will notice how hurt, sensitive, or vulnerable they are. They try to empower through harm because they feel powerless. They want control over someone else because they've felt controlled. It's a need to not feel alone in their misery: "misery loves company." This can be generational. The pattern of abuse can continue from generation to generation until someone makes the decision to break the pattern. Remember the chapter on habits—small adjustments can make big changes and shift the course of generational patterns.

When children are consistently mean or cruel or have behavioural issues (aside from mental health), it almost always stems from things going on or not going on at home or school. Lots of mental health issues come from trauma in our childhood. I'm not saying it's always the parents' fault or that every experience is traumatic. These could be things out of parents' control, like a big move due to a job transfer, or marital breakdown, or an absent parent, or abuse from outside the home. Racism and discrimination can also be traumatic. Having more awareness about mental health has given us the space for people to share their journey and struggles, which helps people to not feel alone. This is a huge step toward growth for all and compassion for what people are going through, which in turn helps people to be kind to one another!

Healthy boundaries means not taking on someone else's unkindness or negativity. You allow what you let in and what you block. Communicate what is okay and not okay!

Align your boundaries with good core values and what serves or impacts you in a positive way, helping you to either be still when needed or progressive and moving forward in those moments of your life. Don't lose sight of the things that are important to you. Everything else, release it! Let go, let God!

"The only people who get
upset about you setting
boundaries are the ones
who were benefiting from
you having none."
—Unknown

There are many types of boundaries. These will depend on the stage of life you're at. It's worth looking deeper into what boundaries are appropriate for you according to where you are and your principles and core values.

Self-care is a big part of your boundaries and an important part of this life. It's a daily battle for me. I find it easy to have compassion for others but not for myself. I'm writing this because my kids may have learned from me to put yourself last while you care for everyone else's needs. This is wrong! I do believe that you must care for yourself so you can be the best for the people around you, so if I do any self-care at all, it's usually because of that statement. Hahaha!

Truthfully, here is the care order for my house. Sometimes I slip myself down a few people, but I really am working on this: God, you, your spouse/partner, your children.

Your relationship with God and your self-care are important so that you can help support others. When you're fully aligned, you are your best self. It's like being in a plane and placing the oxygen mask on yourself first so that you can best help the child or person next to you with their mask.

I'm at a different stage in my life, so it's possible that I see things differently now that I'm older—I mean, wiser. My husband has insisted on "self-caring" our relationship. I love him and thank him for this! I don't think we would be as solid without his insistence and persistence. It's not that I didn't want to take the time for him, I just always felt guilty for taking the time for just the two of us. When the kids were younger and still now, it takes a lot of organizing to get away, regardless of if we're going for a week or a few hours. Taking this time for just us has really made us a strong partnership! You must take time as a couple to build your bond, to become a team, the ultimate partnership, to be the united front, to be able to work together against—I mean to parent—your children! ☺ I'll talk more about this later.

One of my very best friends, one who knows me to my core, told me about Kristen Neff. Kristen Neff has a PhD and has a long list of accomplishments, including books on self-compassion, YouTube videos, Ted talks, etc.

Kristen has a fun self-compassion quiz. I took the quiz and failed! UGH! I strongly dislike failing anything to do with anything. Hmmm, competitive factor again—but especially my own psychology.

> "You have been criticizing yourself for years, and it hasn't worked. Try approving of yourself and see what happens."[25]
> —Louise Hay

---

[25] "Louise Hay Quotes," Quotefancy, accessed November 1, 2024, https://quotefancy.com/quote/854840/Louise-Hay-You-have-been-criticizing-yourself-for-years-and-it-hasn-t-worked-Try.

TAKE TIME

to be still, reflect, listen, journal, and pray.

What boundaries do you need to establish for your well-being? Are you as compassionate to yourself as you are to others? What strategies can help you show more self-compassion?

_____

_____

_____

_____

_____

_____

_____

_____

_____

_____

_____

_____

_____

_____

_____

_____

_____

PRAY

Jesus, please give me a
heart of compassion.
Remove judgement and
criticism of self and
all others. Help me to
set healthy boundaries
that are aligned with
your Word through
love, kindness, and
compassion. Amen!

ALL ABOUT RELATIONSHIPS
Wheel Alignment and a Tune-Up!

*"As iron sharpens iron, so
one person sharpens another"* (Proverbs 27:17).

I am truly a quality-time person. Knowing your partner's "love language" is very helpful toward a successful relationship. Here are the five love languages according to Dr. Gary Chapman:

1. gifts/tokens of affection
2. quality time together
3. physical touch
4. words of affirmation
5. acts of service

There is a test, so have yourself and your partner, family member, child, or friend take this test; it's fun and a

good tool to know one's love language and an excellent starting point.[26]

If you've been with your partner for a long time, you probably already know their love language, or you think you know. You might get some surprises, as the test gives you the order of most important to the least important. Maybe you've been bringing flowers home every week and find out that although that's a nice gesture, your partner prefers acts of service, like a little extra cleaning. Using this for a romantic relationship will allow you to focus on what builds your partner up. You can use this tool to focus on building up any person in any type of relationship, but I'm going to refer more to the romantic side for a moment.

If you're a good match, focusing on your partner's needs will create the desire in your partner to reciprocate your efforts. When one feels loved while the other puts forth effort, the other will want to give love and match that effort in a healthy way. Seeking out help to learn more tools through coaching or counselling with God's guidance will strengthen your bond and foundation.

You will be most successful if you have a partner who complements your personality and character, and vice versa. By complement I mean a soft or gentle opposite, where

---

[26] You can access the test, as of November 2024, at https://5lovelanguages. com/quizzes/.

your values, morals, beliefs, and ideals are aligned but you are different people with different approaches. Where your weakness is their strength, and their weakness is your strength, but not to a detriment or an extreme where you can't find common ground. It's true that opposites attract and work best when they complement each other.

TAKE TIME
to be still, reflect, listen, journal, and pray.

What is your love language? If you have a partner, what is their love language? If you don't have a partner, choose an important relationship to focus on and find out their love language. How can you enhance your connection with them by knowing their love language? How does it help to enhance your relationship to know yours?

_____

_____

_____

_____

_____

_____

_____

_____

_____

_____

RELATIONSHIP FOUNDATION AND FOCUS

What is your foundation? What are you focusing on in your relationship? Are these aligned with your partner? What's important to you both? What are the deal breakers? What is your relationship foundation built on? Whose needs are you focusing on? What happens when you each focus on yourselves? When this happens, neither of you will feel fulfilled. You'll most likely be unhappy and eventually resentful, and you'll start to separate your lives from each other. Regardless of what kind of relationship this is, try to focus on their needs. See what shifts in the relationship.

My marriage foundation is built on the Word of God. It was important to us to be married in a church by a pastor. Now more than ever, we've put God at the centre of our relationship.

A great foundation guide is a book called the Bible. It's the best-selling book of all time and has sold billions of copies. Many archaeological discoveries have validated the historical accuracy of events and locations mentioned in the Bible. The Bible contains various literary genres, including historical narrative, poetry, prophecy, letters, and apocalyptic literature. I find it fascinating! There's no other book like it! History mixed with lessons—does it get any better?

My husband read and worked through a fun book titled *The Love Dare* by Alex Kendrick. It's to be read in secret, unknown to your partner. It's an experiment per say. It was actually incredible how our relationship changed, even though I felt like our relationship was solid. It did make a difference and we did level up from where we were!

It's also important to choose to love the differences in your partner. Couples can fall into the score-keeping rut: "I do this, they don't do that! I always, they never!" This is a relationship strainer. It's like continually chipping away at a weak spot in your foundation. You will weaken the structure. If you catch yourself doing this, stop now. It won't resolve any issues. Inevitably you just continue to repeat the same patterns, never learning, growing, or changing.

You are in control of what you are doing or not doing, saying or not saying. You are in control of your reactions and your focus. You are in control of your thoughts and words. You can choose the path, direction, and focus of all of these. It's a hard practice for some, but making that choice is up to you, and you can do it!

Your partner might not be capable of fulfilling a requested need, or it's not a priority to them. Maybe the task in question is your strength and not theirs. Ask yourself if it's a deal breaker. Communicate to replace the resentment with understanding! Communicate what is important and negotiate. Your partner may not be able to give you exactly what you need, but maybe there's a compromise. A deal breaker is a deal breaker, but if you have agreed, then you need to work through how you can let it go and carry on.

Communication timing is key. During a heated argument isn't always ideal. Schedule a sit-down or a walk when you can talk and things won't get out of control. Stay on topic. I think you'll be surprised at what you find out from your partner and what they're capable of.

Are you listening? Really listening? Eliminate distractions! Set a time slot! Block interruption! Make eye contact! Give your partner your undivided attention. Lean in and toward them. If you have kids, parents, or family members living with you, make sure they're not in the middle of this conversation, as they are a distraction. Put your phone down and turn the TV off.

What is the recurring pattern? How do you change this? Stop focusing on your own needs only. You entered into a partnership, so act like you're in one.

Remember when you entered into this relationship? Remember how you focused on learning as much as you could about your partner? Remember how you listened to them when they talked? Or how they listened to you?

Focus:

1. communicate needs
2. negotiate needs
3. compromise needs

TAKE TIME
to be still, reflect, listen, journal, and pray.

What relationship in your life is a priority? What comes up for you when you think of this relationship? Is there room to learn and grow? How can you deepen the connection? What's the focus? What strategies can be used to communicate what either of you want out of this relationship?

_____

_____

_____

_____

_____

_____

_____

_____

_____

_____

_____

_____

_____

_____

_____

_____

_____

_____

_____

_____

_____

_____

_____

_____

_____

_____

_____

_____

_____

_____

RELATIONSHIP BUILDING IDEAS

Helpful reminders: Greet each other when you arrive home, go to bed together, pray together, give positive affirmation to each other, have regular date nights just the two of you, connect physically and intimately regularly, go away just the two of you a few times per year (weekends), spend time with friends, spend time apart, go to church together. Do things in common together. Try new things together. Try something your partner enjoys. Go watch live music together, like the Dreams 2 Reality Band (shameless plug). Be active together and engage in hobbies together. Make this time a priority. Find your common ground and find something you could learn to love. Take a course or class together. Join a fantasy football league together or separately so that watching football is fun!

I didn't love golf. I found it boring and slow. But I promised my husband that I would work on being decent enough to play golf with him by the time we retired, because he loved it. I got a head start in my forties and found that I loved the peace and quiet of the golf course, away from the business of life, work, and kids. I started taking lessons and now it's a great five-hour date. We go on golf holidays together, and I just love spending that time with Jonn.

I love to paddle board. Jonn didn't want to paddle board due to his lack of balance, but he continued to try it because I loved it. Now he's found his balance and lots of peace. We now have two paddle boards and love this time together.

Figure out what works for the two of you; these are some simple ideas. Being active builds up your mental state, endorphins, and self-esteem, and it helps you to be the best you for those in your life. Some of the best conversation and communication happen during these active moments. It's a distraction that contributes to the ease of communication, unlike external distractions like kids, people, phones, or TV. This is putting self-care into your relationships. It is quality time. Thanks to my husband for taking the lead on this! We go away a few times a year, just the two of us, whether for an overnight date night or a week-long adventure. This helps us to connect and be a better unit, without the distractions, for those who rely on us. If a weekend away and overnights aren't a possibility for you, then make it a weekend together at home. Ask family or friends to take the kids for a few hours or over-night. Hire a babysitter if that's possible. Play games, go for a walk, turn your phones off, do a devotional together, make dinner together, schedule time to be intimate. You will never regret it.

It's important to have self-love and self-care and rid yourself of negativity and self-destruction. You need things that you're passionate about or enjoy doing, or friends you enjoy spending time with, or classes you like to take. I'm talking about in your relationships. If you focus on giving and not what you should get, what you will get is joy!

> "God has given us two hands, one to receive with and the other to give with. We are not cisterns made for hoarding; we are chan-nels made for sharing."[27]
> —Billy Graham

I'm not saying that you shouldn't have a clear idea of what you need from your partner! Focus on what you can control—your behaviour, your patterns, how you show

---

[27] "Billy Graham Quotes," BrainyQuote, accessed November 1, 2024, https://www.brainyquote.com/quotes/billy_graham_150657.

up—and see if that makes a shift. It's important to have clear boundaries and not be taken advantage of, but you are in control of that too. Don't be a victim of your circumstances. Are you being taken advantage of? Time to move on! Is the relationship energy one-sided? All of the above are tools to help change that.

TAKE TIME

to be still, reflect, listen, journal, and pray.

Which of these relationship-building ideas align in your life, and how can you implement strategies to incorporate them into your relationship? How might you both actively support each other's interests?

_____

_____

_____

_____

_____

_____

_____

_____

_____

_____

_____

_____

_____

_____

_____

_____

_____

_____

_____

_____

_____

_____

_____

_____

_____

_____

_____

_____

_____

_____

RELATIONSHIP ASSUMPTION, PRESUMPTION, AND EXPECTATION

Assumption. A thing that's accepted as true or as certain to happen, without proof.

Negative Assumption, in any relationship, is destructive and not proactive. This lacks communication because you're coming to your own conclusion, without any evidence, or you assume an outcome from past experiences. Many times your assumptions are wrong, hurtful, exaggerated, and misguided. Your presumptions come from wounds from the past that have surfaced and have nothing to do with the present moment.

You must let go of expectations regarding other people's actions. There's a fine line here. It's important to have clear boundaries and to communicate what you need from your partner or in any relationship. But are they capable of giving you the things you expect, or are you setting them up to fail continually? You may have to accept the things that they're not capable to give, or come up with a workable compromise that you can live with. Then let it go. Don't dwell on what they can't give you. Ask yourself if it's a deal breaker or not. Stop complaining about your partner, and then continue to stay in the relationship.

Here's a prime example: Your partner can't remember a date that's important to you, like your birthday or anniversary. Ladies, I'm sorry, but stereotypically we do this. We have an expectation and wait for the failure so we can complain about how much the men in our lives don't care. Maybe we need to remind them instead of waiting for them to forget again and not live up to our expectations. This is a set up! Communicate your expectations in advance. Setting up your partner to fail ultimately leads to resentment. You will need to assist in helping this person to become successful, otherwise you'll experience resentment, relationship dissatisfaction, and complaints.

This can also be true for your other relationships, such as with your children regarding expected tasks. Set them up to succeed by reminding them of your expectations. Communication is really the bottom line here. Please note that you can communicate your expectation, and the other person may not be able to live up to your expectation. It's possible that they just don't have the ability, or the relationship isn't a priority for them. If they're willing, this is where negotiation comes into play.

Obviously, if this is the relationship with your child, you can't leave the relationship, so re-focus. You can communicate your expectation to a child, but they may not be as receptive to the execution as you expect. Or their execution may not be the same as you execute the task, so take this into consideration. Some tools may be to write it down in a journal or on a board or in a note. This might have to be repeated several times. I continue to communicate with my kids about my dishwasher expectation. I realized the other day that this form of communication was not effective, so I wrote a large note where they stack their dishes to remind them the location of the dishwasher. Instead of being angry and putting them in the dishwasher myself, I call them back to the kitchen to load it. I'm trying to release my resentment over being overworked with kitchen responsibilities. One day they too will see how wonderful it is to put the dishes in the dishwasher, and how easy it is if everyone simply puts their own dirty dishes in the dishwasher. If the dishes in the dishwasher are clean, it only takes thirty seconds to empty it and then place your dirty dish in the dishwasher! (End rant here!☺) I'll keep you posted on how this turns out. In my experience, kids only really enjoy loading and unloading their own dishwasher when they move out. But really, does anyone like dealing with the dishwasher? The dishwasher might have been a bad example to use for this expectation segment!

TAKE TIME
to be still, reflect, listen, journal, and pray.

How do assumptions, presumptions, and expectations impact your relationships? Can you recall a specific instance where negative assumptions or expectations led to misunderstandings or conflict in your relationship? How could communication have helped prevent or resolve this?

_____

_____

_____

_____

_____

_____

_____

_____

_____

_____

_____

_____

_____

_____

_____

_____

_____

_____

_____

_____

_____

_____

_____

_____

_____

_____

_____

_____

_____

RELATIONSHIP ENERGY

I t's wonderful to have chemistry or passion and to gain
the ability to keep that alive, through focus and attention toward your partner! This is a life-long journey. You can't stop working on your relationships; if you
do, they will suffer and not be fulfilling. Relationships are
most important. If you have solid relationships around
you, and a good support system because you worked on
focusing and putting effort into those relationships, you'll
have solid ground to run toward your goals and dreams.

Stereotypical masculine quality: Want to solve their
partner's problems fast, make the problem smaller, squash
it, fix it, and move on.

Stereotypical feminine quality: Affirm your struggle,
talk about your problem, ask questions, see it as a way to
connect with their partner.

What quality do you possess in your relationships?
Stereotypically again, this is male and female, but I do
believe we all have bits of both, dependent on who the

relationship is with. If you can recognize which traits you and your partner possess, then you can better know how to communicate and come to resolutions.

We are all the human race! We are not where we need to be, but I believe and pray we are moving in the right direction. There is still so much work to do. Having said that, I don't pretend to understand every race's experiences, past or present. I absolutely don't! So I can't speak to this. I only know that I would love to live in a world where we build each other up, work together, and use our skills to make this life fulfilling and full of purpose.

We need to embrace our differences. The lines of communication are opening, but they need to be wider. Some people may never open or widen their lines, but many of us want this desperately. We need this to be the norm. We all need to learn and grow. We can be kinder toward each other. Imagine if we worked together without hate. What would that look like? We can all learn from each other. We are the human race, made up of different races and cultures. How wonderfully diverse! We need to focus on embracing each other's gifts, qualities, and contributions while loving our differences.

The eye cannot say to the hand, "I have no need of

you," nor again the head to the feet, "I have no need of you." But quite the contrary, the parts of the body that seem to be weaker are [absolutely] necessary; and as for those parts of the body which we consider less honorable, these we treat with greater honor; and our less presentable parts are treated with greater modesty ...
(1 Corinthians 12:21–23, AMP)

Honestly, I keep trying to cut it off, but it's just plain as day! You have a purpose! You are important! God said so!

... while our more presentable parts do not require it. But God has combined the [whole] body, giving greater honor and to that part which lacks it, so that there would

be no division or discord
in the body [that is, lack of
adaption of the parts to each
other], but that the parts
may have the same concern
for one another.
(1 Corinthians 12:24–25,
AMP)

We're called to be loving, kind, forgiving, compassionate, and humble to each other. We're not to be fearful,
anxious, conceited, or boastful. Who doesn't want to be
aligned with that?!

PUTTING THE WORD TO WORK

Do you ever feel like your
spiritual gifts are not as important as someone else's?
That's like saying your eyes
are not as important as your
ears. The truth is every gift
is necessary for the body of
Christ to function as God
intends. (See 1 Corinthians
12:20-25) Recognize and

celebrate the importance of
each person's gifts, including
your own. However, be sure
not to think more highly
of your gifts than someone
else's.[28]

This means we all have a part to play. We are all important to the body of Christ and the successful functioning of society. All members of the body have a purpose. One is not above the other. We need each other to fulfill our potential and purpose.

And if one member suffers,
all the parts share the suffering; if one member is honored, all rejoice with it. Now
you [collectively] are Christ's
body, and individually [you
are] members of it [each with
his own special purpose and
function]. (1 Corinthians
12:26–27, AMP).

---

[28] The Every Day Bible (New York, NY: Warner Faith, 2006), 1867.

Not everyone can be a teacher or a manager or a trades person or a doctor or an engineer. God gave us all gifts and a purpose to use those gifts. To create unity among us, we must accept each other. Differences are beautiful! Inside and out! Imagine a world where we were all the same, with the same gifts and abilities and purpose. Boring! We have only one unified purpose, and that is to seek after God through accepting Jesus as Saviour. Beyond that, we are created to be different, with different purposes and gifts. Why do we continue to criticize, judge, and shame each other for our differences? How is this productive? How has this served us? Diversity is beautiful, so let's embrace each other and our differences. God does!

There are no two fingerprints the same. There are no two DNA patterns or sequences the same. Pretty amazing! How does that just explode into existence? You are fearfully and wonderfully made in His image (Psalm 139:14). Each our own very unique self! How can we lift each other up and see the value we each possess? I think if we started doing this, people would start to live with purpose and joy. Not everyone's purpose is career-focused or job-oriented. Sometimes your purpose is to support. Embrace and love who you are from your inside to your outside, and the gifts you've been given.

Is there a limiting story that needs to be eliminated? How do you change that story? Start by asking yourself how you are showing up in your relationships.

TAKE TIME
to be still, reflect, listen, journal, and pray.

Reflecting on the concept of unity within diversity as discussed in 1 Corinthians 12, explain how can you apply this principle to your relationships, both inside and outside your immediate circle.

_____

_____

_____

_____

_____

_____

_____

_____

_____

_____

_____

_____

PRAY

God, thank you for my
relationship with you!
Guide me to strengthen
that first. Help me to put
what I learn from you
into practice in all my
relationships. Help me to
choose positive thoughts
and to focus and choose
kindness and forgiveness.
Help me to show love
and embrace differences
in people. Help me to see
what you love in people.
Guide me to build strong
foundations that create
healthy relationships.
Amen!

FEARFULLY AND WONDERFULLY MADE

Superior Design, Excellence Redefined!

"For we are God's handiwork, created in Christ Jesus to do good works, which God prepared in advance for us to do" (Ephesians 2:10).

Do babies come out with a predisposed life path or character regardless of their upbringing or circumstances? Why are children raised in the same home yet turn out different from each other? How does a child raised in an abusive environment follow the pattern, while another in the same situation chooses to break the pattern and take a different path? Some children are raised in a safe environment with healthy boundaries, but they choose to self-destruct. If those kids find their way and thankfully come out of it, is it because of what happened while going through the self-destructive stage? Or is it simply luck of the draw that they made it? Did they lean into their faith? My husband and I often have talked about the fact that we made it through those teen years, while people we knew in the same neighbourhood did not. Was it because of our parents? Our own character? Our circumstances? Our choices? Our focus?

In some families, the parents' lives revolve around substance abuse, but their children don't use substances; instead, they're focused on sports or activities, school, or work. Why is that? Other families have a hard rule about no drugs in their house; they are active and healthy, but their children use and seem depressed, or they self-harm and feel like their life is inadequate. Why do some kids raised in tough, poor neighbourhoods, where they witness tragedy daily, rise up and become super successful, while others live a life of crime? Then others raised in neighbourhoods with little to no crime struggle to make it. How are some people's kids super smart in school when they themselves didn't do well in school? What did those parents do different?

I saw a post on Instagram. It was a picture of two men. One was a drunk with a sign that said, "No money, no job." The other was an ambitious, successful businessman. When asked why they'd walked the path they did, they both gave the same reason: their fathers were alcoholics. The only difference was their character and then choices. One became the victim of their circumstance and continued with the generational curse, and the other used their circumstances as motivational fuel and broke the generational chains. This can also happen in the same family.

I believe this is because God created you to be unique in His image with your own purpose. But you start out created by God with your very own soul, spirit, original DNA sequence, character, and plan: "*'For I know the plans and thoughts that I have for you,' says the Lord, 'plans for peace and well-being and not for disaster, to give you a future and a hope*" (Jeremiah 29:11, AMP).

I haven't talked about the devil much in this book. I used to not even be able to discuss the enemy from my own fear. He is the great deceiver, a total liar. The devil works hard to ruin God's plan, to throw you off course. But we have free will to make choices and choose our focus in our lives. We can fall victim to our circumstances, allowing our tragedy or trauma to control and guide our outcome, or we can use our circumstances to control our choices and reactions.

We will have trials living in this world, but you don't need to go through these alone. If we didn't have trials, we wouldn't learn and grow. Some people's circumstances are debilitating and unspeakable. The devil wants you to fall victim to these. Flick him off like the flea he is! I'm not saying this is an easy feat. What I am saying is to lean into God. He is bigger, greater, and more powerful than the enemy! He will comfort you, give you peace, and pull you through. Align yourself with God and fight against the devil for what is already rightfully yours from birth. God doesn't want you to be a victim of your circumstances. God wants you to heal and live a glorious life. If you focus on being a victim, then that's what you'll be.

You can choose to work on healing! Reframe to a positive focus! Seek God, seek guidance! Do whatever it takes—forgive, find your gratitude, pray, read the Word, get counselling or coaching, start training. This gives your purpose a chance to shine.

> Oh yes, you shaped me first inside, then out; you formed me in my mother's womb. I thank you, High God—you're breathtaking! Body and soul, I am

marvelously made! I worship in adoration—what a creation! You know me inside and out, you know every bone in my body; you know exactly how I was made, bit by bit, how I was sculpted from nothing into something. Like an open book, you watched me grow from conception to birth; all stages of life were spread out before you, the days of my life all prepared before I'd even lived one day.

(Psalm 139:13–16, MSG)

TAKE TIME

to be still, reflect, listen, journal, and pray.

Considering that we are all *"fearfully and wonderfully made"* with a unique purpose by God, how have you seen your own life circumstances—whether challenging or supportive—shape your character and choices? Have you leaned into your faith or personal strengths to overcome obstacles and/or fulfill your purpose?

_____

_____

_____

_____

_____

_____

_____

_____

_____

_____

_____

_____

_____

_____

_____

PRAY IN THANKSGIVING

Thank you, God, that
I am fearfully and
wonderfully made! Help
me see what you saw
when you created me.
Thank you that you have
a plan and purpose for my
life. Thank you that you
have plans for peace and
well-being and not for
disaster! Thank you that
you give me hope. I cast
out and block, in your
name, the whispered lies
of the enemy. Amen!

SAME HOUSE: DIFFERENT KIDS/ DIFFERENT RULES
Unique Destination, Identical Road!

> *For just as each of us has one body with many members, and these members do not all have the same function, so in Christ we, though many, form one body, and each member belongs to all the others. We have different gifts, according to the grace given to each of us.*
>
> (Romans 12:4-6a)

M y mom is the third of six girls in her family. She says her parents were harder on her oldest sister, but also that by watching how her parents reacted to her sister, she learned quickly what not to do. She wasn't an angel—she just learned how to hide things from her parents so as not to worry them. I think her parents, my grandparents, appreciated that. They may have just been tired, as they had six daughters all around the older teen, teen, and pre-teen years. The fact they survived is actually amazing!

Maybe I too was harder on my oldest daughter when she was a teenager than I was on my middle son and youngest daughter. You learn with your first child what's important to you as a parent and how to achieve it. Then you take what you learned and apply it to the next children in line, only to find out that they are completely different and those rules don't apply.

My children are five years and then four years apart. They are different people and their situations and choices have been mostly different, but they have walked some of the same path. When each of them was little, we learned quickly that they required different rules, and not because they were different sexes. I had to have a stronger hold on my son versus my oldest daughter as toddlers because he was a runner, and she never was. She wouldn't go with a stranger, but she would just stay in the same spot. She was content to sit with me or with whomever. She was, and still is, our social butterfly. Therefore, I was more relaxed with her freedoms when we were out. I said good luck to the person who tried to take my son, as he was a runner. He loved to look at you and then take off running, fully laughing and having the time of his life, but he wasn't going with anyone either. He would have turned very quickly from fun-loving into a full-on fighter.

Chelsey would participate in every class she took, sitting nicely in the circle, paying attention. Before we had our next two children, Jonn and I thought we were really good at this parenting thing. We gave her our expectations for behaviour in certain situations, and she followed it to the letter. She was so easy to manage and care for.

Our son had the same expectations given to him, but he was a runner. At three years old I put him in swimming lessons. All the parents watched from behind the glass, not on the pool deck. Joel and I talked about this prior to class, along with the expectations for him joining this class. I told him he must listen to the teacher and follow her instruction. This would have been all I needed to say to Chels. During the class, Joel started to dive bomb under the water for all the toys at the bottom of the pool, while all the other kids in the class where nicely blowing bubbles. Clearly Joel's swimming comfort level was above the class we'd signed him up for.

This young swim instructor, bless her kind heart, couldn't get him to blow bubbles and join the circle. I was motioning to him through the glass to join the class, and the teacher tried to softly coax him back to the circle. He just kept diving down and grabbing another ring from the bottom and shooting up with a huge smile to proudly show me what he'd accomplished. I went on the pool deck and firmly told him that his choices were to participate or get out of the pool. This now flustered young lady was not assertive and didn't know how to deal with Joel's energy. She looked defeated and kept looking at me to do something. He was having the time of his life. I told Joel if he didn't join the teacher, he would have to get out. All of this was super disruptive to the class, and I could feel the glares of the other parents. And then the head lifeguard came to me and said I needed to get him out of the pool if he wouldn't join the class. We've laughed about this story over the years.

The next thing that happened sent me over the "embarrassing parenting moment" edge. I went out on the pool deck again, and in front of all the staring parents, I told Joel this was his final chance to join the class. So what did he do? He dove back under the water. Then I said, "Okay, out of the pool." But each time I called his name, he dove under before I could finish my sentence.

Oh my gosh! This child! Meanwhile, the head lifeguard was yelling at me to get him out of the pool, that it wasn't safe for him to be that far from his instructor. I did finally get him out once I was in a full sweat. I took him out of lessons until his age matched his pool comfort and the lesson plans provided.

Life lesson here: Let's support and choose kindness and compassion for parents or caregivers as they navigate the high energy child. Most of us are blessed with at least one! ☺

I saw a grandma in the grocery store with three young grandsons. The oldest was having a very loud meltdown over something she had said no to. I could feel and see the heat of her body rising in embarrassment as she tried to keep herself and him calm. As people stared, she left the store, struggling to manage the cart and three little guys.

I walked over to her and said, "Please let me help you take the younger boys to your car. I have kids, and I know exactly what you're going through. You're doing a great job; stick with it. She said, "Yes please" with a smile of relief on her face. This gave her a new energy and space to be able to deal with this little guy and give him the attention he needed. This gave me the opportunity to tell his brothers what a great help they were to their grandma, ensuring that their patient behaviour didn't go unnoticed. Kindness and compassion at work.

Joel always wanted to fight and wrestle. Chelsey wanted to sit, play quietly, and talk. Hailey is a total combo of the two of them. She would snuggle with Chels but then playfight with Joel. Always trying to make everyone laugh.

As different as my kids are, they all battled mental health stuff in the teen years. I continually try to give all my kids life skills and direction to help them lead their best life. Of course, they have choices and free will; they are their own people. They all made different choices, as they are different people and want different things. We are in the teen years with our third child. She too will choose her path. I pray that we have taught her and prepared her enough to navigate high school.

As a parent, we learn from our first child and realize the things that work and the things we should let go of. Learning and growing! You realize as you navigate parenting that your first child is so different than your second, and your third, and that each of them has their own path. Your responsibility as a parent is to guide and correct them as they find their way in a healthy direction toward their purpose-filled life! This is why as parents we need to learn, grow, and adjust.

I said to our oldest, "How could Dad and I have done things differently, now that you're an adult?" All three struggled with mental health issues. She said, "We were going to go through these things anyway. Maybe God gave us to you because He knew you'd guide and teach us. Your life lessons made me who I am and brought me safely out the other side. You think I wasn't listening, but it's actually what saved me." Wow! When your child validates your relentless life lessons in the car talks and spouts wisdom!

My mom always told me that you teach them all you can, baby to preteen years. During the teen years, you hold on tight to them. Don't let go and they'll come back to you. Don't give up! Keep building the relationship with them. This is the time they want to be the furthest from you, but they actually need you the most. And not surprisingly, there is a scripture for this: "*Train up a child in the way he should go [teaching him to seek God's wisdom and will for his abilities and talents], even when he is old he will not depart from it*" (Proverbs 22:6, AMP).

They might step back from this good training while they navigate these tough years, trying to find themselves and who they are, feeling like independents but still growing into adults. They're managing hormonal changes, physical changes, and brain development. They will come back to that good training—just continue to hold tight. Don't give up, and seek help when help is needed. Pray! I believe they are trying to find themselves and their place and purpose in this world.

Home life and the people they surround themselves with are big factors for sure. Make home a safe, warm space for them. Pray for them always, every day! Pray for the Holy Spirit to fill your home with love and peace. There are plenty of non-peaceful things outside the home. Continue to love them when they walk through the door. It's a choice!

My youngest spouted off tools and a life lesson in the car again when I was having a tough day and needed a reminder! I was overthinking about a situation I had no control over. She said, "Mom, you don't have any control over what this person says or does; you can't take that on. You can only control your own reaction to it, so don't give it any weight or it will bring you down."

I said, "Wow, you've been listening!"

"Yes," she said, "of course I'm listening!"

Another time she informed me, again in the car, where some of the best conversations happen, that she thinks her dad and I are pretty reasonable parents. She said she feels like she can tell us things and we won't completely freak out. Our oldest believes that our youngest, Hailey, has her to thank for this, and she's likely right! Listen, validate, negotiate, communicate, advise, and guide. Not always in that order. I appreciate so much that she talks to us. Keep the communication lines open so they feel like it's a safe space for them to share. I tell my kids that it doesn't mean we will always be agreeable, but we will always be open to a conversation. And we have learned what to focus on from the experience of parenting her sister and brother. Being the third or fourth child, you get the best version of your parents. Now my two daughters and my son all guide and teach each other through different situations and life's bumps, using the life lessons they heard in the car. It's pretty amazing to watch! So if you think they aren't listening to you, they really are! Hang on tight! Don't give up! Build your relationship on the rock, not sand.

I love the story my mom shared of when she was a teen and was out of control, yelling at her parents. Her father put his arm around her mother and said, "Come on, dear, another one going through the difficult stage." They turned and went into their room and closed the door. We have laughed so hard about this. They were so wise, or quite simply worn down. I just love the calmness of their reaction.

Sometimes not reacting or freaking out is required in the immediate moment to de-escalate. Then the communication can happen later. Sometimes taking a minute to gather your thoughts so that your words can be constructive is required. Most times communication that starts with yelling is not productive. When you have taken that moment in time to breathe, calm your nervous system, and pray, you can then listen, hear, and have productive communication and continue to build your relationship with your child.

TAKE TIME
to be still, reflect, listen, journal, and pray.

As a child, did you have different rules for each sibling in
your house? If you are an only child, like me, did your parents instill different rules than when they were brought up?
In your opinion, were they appropriately suited to your
personality? If you are a parent or a caregiver, do you find
yourself adapting the rules for different children?

_____

_____

_____

_____

_____

_____

_____

_____

_____

_____

PRAY

Lord, give me the
wisdom, guidance,
compassion, and love I
need to support and/or
care for others, whether
it be children, mentally
or physically challenged
people, or the elderly.
Help me to love like you
love, give guidance like
you guide, be wise like
you are wise, be strong
like you are strong, be
kind like you are kind,
have peace like you
have peace, have joy like
you have joy, and have
compassion and empathy
like you have. Help me to
be more like you, Jesus!
Amen!

MOST IMPORTANT LIFE LESSON
Study the Map and Navigate the Streets!

> *"... I am the way and the truth and the life. No one comes to the Father except through me"* (John 14:6).

The most important lesson we can pass on to our children—to all children and their descendants for generations—is to emulate Jesus! That really covers everything you want to teach your children. Jesus did live and He lived a life without sin, as told in the Bible. It's historically accurate.

Be an example as you walk your walk and talk your talk in everything you do, and in how you react and show up, with God as your guide. Build your foundation on rock, not sand. Build a relationship with God and drop the religious rules. Your guide is His Word. It's all there in scripture, in the Bible. We will never be perfect, but we aren't required to be. Jesus was for us.

Don't you think it's interesting that we are drawn to having relationships? You were created to be in relationship with each other, so doesn't it make sense that God would want His own relationship with you? You will be filled with purpose, peace, hope, and joy. Invite Jesus into your heart. You have nothing to lose and an eternity of love and joy to gain.

God is light and all about loving you. He is your creator and is already in you. You simply need to invite Him into your heart and accept that Jesus died on the cross for you to wash away your sins so you can spend eternity in heaven with Him. It's a simple prayer. See the end of the book for the prayer of salvation.

MOST IMPORTANT LIFE LESSON

TAKE TIME

to be still, reflect, listen, journal, and pray.

Where are you in your faith journey? How can you mimic Jesus and make it relatable in today's world? How can you build a foundation of faith in your daily life? How will this affect your interactions with others?

_____

_____

_____

_____

_____

_____

_____

_____

_____

_____

_____

199

_____

_____

PRAY

Dear Lord, please provide
me with discernment
and wisdom to guide
our next generation
to walk with you, talk
with you, learn from
you, and grow through
you. To give them tools
to cope and healthy
communication skills. To
live in love and not hate,
to choose positive focus
and thoughts. To live in
kindness and forgiveness.
To have compassion for
one another. And most
importantly, to put their
relationship with you first!
Amen!

EVERYONE SHOULD STARFISH!
Pump the Brakes!

*Do not fear [anything], for
I am with you; do not be
afraid, for I am your God.
I will strengthen you, be
assured I will help you; I
will certainly take hold of
you with My righteous right
hand [a hand of justice, of
power, of victory, of salva-
tion].* (Isaiah 41:10, AMP)

Our family went through something that changed the course of our lives. Challenging times mentally and physically. Then God called us back again! Through and during this time, we made the decision to use our circumstances as motivational fuel to go back to church and put God first. We never walked away from God, but we definitely weren't walking with Him—more like running ahead and trying to find fulfilment on our own. We weren't fully trusting in Him, and we didn't put Him first. The difference in my life from then to now is indescribable! I am full of hope and peace! We are called to be in fellowship and be in church, to plug in, to worship, to have relationships.

During this time there was a plethora of stressful situations happening in our family, from mental health issues due to work situations to needing to take a step back and change directions. My mom and son were sick, and we were dealing with rejection and people we loved walking out of our lives. In the midst of all of that, we had so much love and support from friends and family. I can't even tell these people how they helped pull us through all of this. I've mentioned a few in this book. You think you shouldn't bother someone when they're going through a tough time, but when you get the nudge, follow through with it! Let's support and love each other!

Our brothers and sisters in Christ walked with us, prayed for us, let us lean on them, showed us how to dial back into our faith or, for me, to even have faith at all! Our kids have formed a generational bond. They have walked with each other through some of the darkest times—

through mental and physical health challenges! They prayed, believed, protected, read scripture, spent quality time, had kitchen dance parties, served in and attended church together, and bonded over books, football, and loving God. It's truly amazing!

A few very big things happened during the storm that can only be explained through the love of God. For myself, I felt that nudge to find and work with a life coach.

Our family focused on God and got back into reading His Word; we got rooted back to our faith, prayed, and found a home church again. This was thanks to our oldest daughter, who had said a few months prior that we needed to get back to church. She was absolutely right! We had church hopped for years and then slowly fell away from going at all. We tried doing life on our own and we were falling apart.

Then our friends invited us to This is Life Church, now River Valley Church Vancouver. We went, and we have not left! We are home! I knew this for two reasons. There was that warm, safe feeling again, which is fully the presence of the Holy Spirit. It's when you walk into a space and you feel love. You feel peace. You feel protection. You feel acceptance. And the heartbeat of this church is "Love God, Love People, Love Life!" They are a full five-fold ministry, teaching the Word of God from the

Bible. All their signage, website, and "church merch," as our youngest, Hailey, says, has #lovepeople written on it. This is aligned with God and my true self!

River Valley Church Vancouver's core values:

> Relationship over Religion
> Grace over Judgement
> Character over Gifting
> Making a difference as we
> LOVE PEOPLE

This is exactly in line with what I've shared in this book.

We have banded together tightly, as a family should. But I feel superabundantly blessed by this because I know it could have gone the other way. Families can fall apart through a storm. I am so very grateful because it could have torn us apart. For this I give glory to God! We are tighter and stronger through the love and grace of God, now more than ever. In the middle of the storm, our kids have a bond that runs deep. They've all faced challenging situations, and they can relate to each other and help each other survive. At the end of the day, what you have is your relationships with each other and with God.

The girls held our son's head above water when he wasn't able to keep afloat himself and when he was in the pit of darkness, his worst nightmare, his storm. God gave him hope, forgiveness, peace, love, and joy. Then the two oldest held up the youngest as she was so affected mentally by the stormy waters surrounding our family. We are a team, a unit! We have wrapped our arms around each other and pulled in tight.

The final thing happened to me: I "starfished!" And that was the true beginning of my healing. A revelation happened within me! I found true faith! I realized that I didn't have true faith. I say "true" because I realized that I hadn't fully surrendered. When I "starfished," I fully surrendered to God's will! I gave everything to Him! Let go, let God!

Starfish? you ask. I was in a super low, super fearful, super anxiety-filled and scary point of my life, desperate to escape my own feelings and pain from the situations going on around me. I am truly affected by the well-being of my family and friends. I called my husband while having debilitating anxiety. He said, "Go upstairs and get on your knees; pray and give it all to God. I'm on my way!"

I know he said other things, but I can't recall what they were. So I went upstairs and started to pray, and I felt like it wasn't enough. I had only ever prayed on my knees once before, and I felt like more needed to be done. This was not enough. I needed to go bigger. I lay on my bed, face to the heavens with arms wide open and legs out, lying like a starfish. I said, "Take me, Lord. I am yours!" I put on the song on "I Surrender." With tears running down my cheeks, and while singing the words, I spoke out loud, "Take me and use me as you will! I cannot do this without you! I cannot do life without your grace. I will not do this life without you again. I need your love. I need your forgiveness. I need your peace. I need your joy! You promise all of these things. I will do my part. I fully surrender! I cannot do this life alone without you at the centre! I need you, Lord! I have faith and I will trust in you, Lord!"

I let go and I let God! Surrendering is trusting in God to have full control, to let go of my own control. To know and have faith that I have safety walking with Him. To be free from anxiety, worry, and fear. To know that I deserve to feel joy and peace because that's God's will for me and for everyone. I felt peace like I hadn't felt in months. I felt the warmth of the Holy Spirit wash over me. I felt joy! An absolutely incredible "Holy Spirit" moment and turning point for me in the middle of a storm.

As I shared this with my friend Adele, she brought up the starfish moment, making funny comments, and adding it to many of our conversations about life's struggles and storms. This is when I realized just how significant that moment was in my journey. A pivotal moment, a turning point. It's not that I didn't know what I was doing meant, but it just felt so natural and normal, like it wasn't a big deal, even though it was a big deal. And in the middle of their family's storm, she also starfished and gave it all to God! And then she said, "I think everyone should starfish!" Oh my gosh! I love this! And that's exactly it! In those moments, the only way to find true peace is to starfish! God says to surrender, to trust, to have faith and cast your cares onto Him! It really is the natural order of how we were created. Lean on, rely on Him!

Adele sent me the most beautiful text about the celestial symbolism for a starfish: *A starfish represents infinite divine love*! (Wow) *The starfish holds characteristics of guidance, vigilance, inspiration, brilliance, and intuition.*

And my tattoo was created and imbedded on my arm forever and ever. Amen!

TAKE TIME
to be still, reflect, listen, journal, and pray.

What have you willingly surrendered to in your life? Are you open to surrendering? How do you think surrendering could benefit you?

_____

_____

_____

_____

_____

_____

_____

_____

_____

_____

_____

_____

_____

_____

_____

_____

_____

_____

_____

_____

_____

_____

_____

_____

_____

PRAY

Help me to know when
and how to surrender to
your will and purpose for
my life. Amen!

SALVATION

Rugged off-roads,
Tree-lined boulevards,
Fast-paced highways.
Salvation awaits,
No matter the road
you're on.

*"For God so loved the
world, that he gave his only
Son, that whoever believes
in him should not perish
but have eternal life."*
(John 3:16, ESV)

Do you want to enter into a personal relationship with Jesus Christ? It will be the most important and valued relationship you'll ever have! Do you want to feel His love, peace, joy, and grace for eternity in heaven, where there is no pain or suffering, enjoying all the fruits of the Spirit? Existing in the warmth and light of the Holy Spirit? God has given us free will, so we can choose to invite Him into our hearts and receive salvation, or we can choose to walk alone. Heaven is spending eternity with God, and because He's a gracious God, He doesn't force us into a relationship with Him. He didn't create robots. We have choices in all things. We have control over our actions and reactions. We can spend eternity feeling His love, a love that we can't imagine, or we can spend eternity separate from God and His love. God won't force you into a relationship with Him, much like you can't force someone to love you if they don't want to.

If you would like to receive Jesus as your Lord and Saviour, I'm elated for you! You will not regret it! You have nothing to lose and everything to gain!

Please pray this prayer of salvation out loud:

Father God,

Thank you that you sent your only Son to die for me, to wash away my sins. I believe Jesus Christ died on the cross and rose again and is alive in heaven at your right hand. I acknowledge that I am a sinner. I repent of my sins and ask for your forgiveness. I believe Jesus is my Lord and Saviour, and I invite you into my heart. I want to trust in you, Jesus. I want to enter into a personal relationship with you. I want to walk with you. I ask for salvation so I can be with you for eternity. Thank you for hearing my prayer! Amen!

"Peace I leave with you; my peace I give you. I do not give you as the world gives. Do not let your hearts be troubled and do not be afraid" (John 14:27).

If you took a leap of faith, yahoo! Congratulations! Your life is going to change. You never have to be alone! I encourage you to tell someone, such as a Christian friend or family member. Don't do the Christian life alone! Find a faith community!

If you already had salvation, then you know what I'm talking about.

If you're not ready to invite Jesus in, then go back and read the book again. ☺ Just kidding! My prayer is that you feel God's love and that in time you will give your life to Christ.

"Trust [confidently] in Him at all times, O people; pour out your hearts before Him. God is a refuge for us. Selah" (Psalm 62:8, AMP).

> So, I give my life over to Jesus and celebrities ask me questions constantly. This one celebrity said, explain

God to me and I can't, but this is what I came up with. His question was, how is it I can do all of these things that I'm doing, and you still say Jesus wants relationship with me? How is that possible?

This is all that I could come up with at the time and it's not even how awesome God is. I was like, God is kind of like being in the car with the navigation device. If it says go three lights and turn left, then you go one street and turn right, it doesn't abandon what you're supposed to do, it recalculates what you need to do to get to where you're supposed to be based upon where you currently are. Only problem is if you keep making the wrong turns the road conditions will be different. They may be rougher and you're running out of time, so you have to be sensitive to listen to that voice. You can make the right choice about where you're supposed to be.[29]

This entire book is to the glory of God! God had a plan, and now I see why it took so long to finish it. I needed to be fully aligned with Him and myself. I had to know who I was and work through my own battles, which brought me closer to Jesus. I will say it again: God said all this first. Really! The Bible is the OG of self-help books!

OG: Original Gansta—slang term for someone who is incredibly exceptional, authentic or "old-school." OG was originally used in gang culture, but now used as a general term to praise someone who is an expert at something.[30] AKA the Father, the Son, and the Holy Spirit!

[29] First.Free.Church, "So I give my life over to Jesus," Instagram, https://www.instagram.com/reel/CwOG-vxoRnL/?igsh=MW5mNzc1cnNzb2V-leg%3D%3D, paraphrased.
[30] Dictionary.com, s.v. "O.G.," accessed November 1, 2024, https://www.dictionary.com/e/slang/og/.

In the Bible, He gave us all the tools we need to live a fulfilled life. It all comes from Him! He gave me the words, but most of all, the supportive people, family, and friends I needed to finish this book, and I am truly grateful!

> Then Jesus said to his disciples, "Whoever wants to be my disciple must deny themselves and take up their cross and follow me. For whoever wants to save their life will lose it, but whoever loses their life for me will find it.
> (Matthew 16:24–25)

TAKE TIME

to be still, reflect, listen, journal, and pray.

What were the pivotal moments or experiences in your life that shaped your understanding of faith? How do you envision your life changing if you fully embrace a personal relationship with Jesus Christ? What are the ways you can draw closer to Him daily?

_____

_____

_____

_____

_____

_____

_____

_____

_____

_____

_____

_____

_____

_____

_____

_____

_____

PRAY

Thank you, God, for
saving me. Help me to
understand what a fully
committed relationship
feels like with you. Show
me what it means to
lean in, trust, and have
faith in you. Help me to
understand the meaning
of salvation. Let me hear
your soft whisper of
wisdom and purpose for
my life. Amen!

WRAPPING IT UP!
Driving It Home!

> *"The Lord bless you and*
> *keep you; the Lord make his*
> *face to shine upon you and*
> *be gracious to you; the Lord*
> *lift up his countenance upon*
> *you and give you peace"*
> (Numbers 6:24–26, ESV).

A friend sent a text to our small group about the meaning of this blessing, "*the Lord make his face shine upon you.*" It signifies divine favour, grace, and blessing. It means that God is looking upon you with approval and kindness, and His presence is with you. This expression conveys a deep sense of God's benevolence and a close, personal relationship with Him. It implies that you are under His care and that He is bestowing His grace, peace, and blessings upon your life. So beautiful and interesting!

Jonn sent the Ten Toes this amazing Tik Tok from pastor and writer Steven Furtick, and it truly sums up my book! In this Tik Tok, he says that the enemy is so smart, he can get you to make little choices that can compromise who you are. Those little choices can become tomorrow's chains that keep you miserable and weighed down. If he can get you to make the choice once, then he can get you to choose it again. You make a choice to lie. It's just a little choice and it's just a little lie. But choices become habits when you choose them over and over again. You become what you repeatedly do. Then your choice becomes automatic and it's not even a choice anymore. It's gone beyond a choice and a habit and now it's my identity, my nature. While I was making little choices, my chains became huge over time. Chains of anger, anxiety, worry, fear. Practice doesn't make perfect; practice makes permanent.[31]

Your choices affect your entire life. Choose to be grateful, choose to be kind, choose to forgive, choose to love, choose to be humble, choose positive focus, choose to cast out your fears and negative thoughts. Most importantly, choose to lean on, rely on, and trust in God!

[31] "Pastor Steven Furtick: How the Enemy Works," YouTube Short, accessed November 12, 2024, https://www.youtube.com/shorts/UsBJCW9Sxqg.

TAKE TIME
to be still, reflect, listen, journal, and pray.

What part of this book resonated with you most? Is there a positive lesson or takeaway? What practices will you incorporate after reading this book?

_____

_____

_____

_____

_____

_____

_____

_____

_____

_____

_____

_____

_____

_____

_____

_____

_____

_____

_____

_____

_____

_____

_____

_____

_____

_____

_____

_____

_____

_____

_____

_____

_____

MY PRAYER FOR YOU

Lord God, thank you for
the person reading my
book. May they find true
fulfillment in their life.
I pray for their healthy
relationships, including
one with you. I pray
that they will choose
positive focus and let
go of limiting beliefs
through reframing their
thoughts. If they battle
fear and anxiety, Lord,
I pray you release them
of this, and that they
know it's okay to not be
okay. That they choose
kindness, compassion,
and forgiveness. That they
sit in gratitude every day.
That *Life Lessons from
the Car* gave them what
they needed. That this
book made them laugh

while giving them tools
and, most importantly,
life lessons. That they
know they are not alone.
I pray that they clearly
see that even though we
go through trials and
tribulations, we have a
choice on how we show
up and what we focus on.
These choices aren't always
the easy route, but we can
lean on you for guidance,
assurance, and hope. That
they learned and grew. In
Jesus' name. Amen!

SCRIPTURE LIST

#LOVEPEOPLE:
- Proverbs 20:5
- Ephesians 4:32

MY DISCLAIMER:
- Ephesians 4:25
- Philippians 4:13
- Romans 10:9–13
- James 2:26
- Matthew 7:1–4

USEFUL TOOLS:
- James 1:22
- Hebrews 1:14
- Deuteronomy 31:8
- Philippians 4:6–7

BUILDING FULFILLMENT:
- Proverbs 24:3–4
- John 15:12

PHYSICAL WELLNESS:
- 3 John 1:2
- 1 Corinthians 10:31

CHOICES AND FOCUS
- Philippians 4:8
- Habakkuk 2:2–3
- John 16:33
- 1 Peter 5:7

ACTIVELY PERSONAL:
- Isaiah 40:31

MENTAL WELLNESS:
- 1 Corinthians 13:4–5

HABITS: THE GOOD, THE BAD, THE UGLY:
- Psalm 40:2
- Psalm 46:1
- Isaiah 40:29

CHOOSE GRATITUDE:
- 1 Thessalonians 5:18
- Matthew 7:24–27

ANXIETY:
- James 1:2–4
- 2 Timothy 1:7

- Psalm 34:4
- Matthew 18:20

CHOOSE TO BE THE LEADER OF YOUR LIFE:
- Galatians 6:4–5
- 1 Corinthians 12:17
- 1 Corinthians 12:18–21

CHOOSE CONFIDENCE OVER ARROGANCE:
- Philippians 2:3–4
- Matthew 5:5

CHOOSE KINDNESS:
- John 13:34–35
- Colossians 3:12
- Ephesians 4:2–3

CHOOSE FORGIVENESS:
- Colossians 3:13
- Matthew 8:21
- Matthew 6:12

BOUNDARIES AND BEHAVIOURS, PERSPECTIVE AND COMPASSION:
- Romans 12:9–10

ALL ABOUT RELATIONSHIPS:
- Proverbs 27:17
- 1 Corinthians 12:21–23

- 1 Corinthians 12:24–25
- 1 Corinthians 12:26–27

FEARFULLY AND WONDERFULLY MADE:
- Ephesians 2:10
- Jeremiah 29:11
- Psalm 139:13–16

SAME HOUSE, DIFFERENT KIDS/DIFFERENT RULES:
- Romans 12:4–6
- Proverbs 22:6

MOST IMPORTANT LIFE LESSON:
- John 14:6

EVERYONE SHOULD STARFISH:
- Isaiah 41:10

SALVATION:
- John 3:16
- John 14:27
- Psalm 62:8
- Matthew 16:24–25

WRAPPING IT UP:
- Numbers 6:24–26